Depressions'
Child

ALSO BY PERRY L. ANGLE

Existential Musing of a Southern Individualist

Existential Ramblings of a Southern Individualist

The Butterfly Transport

Prophet's Way

An Investment Primer for New Investors

The Waiting Room Chronicles

All are available on iuniverse.com or amazon.com.

Depressions' Child

PERRY L. ANGLE

DEPRESSIONS' CHILD

iUniverse books may be ordered through booksellers or by contacting:

iUniverse
1663 Liberty Drive
Bloomington, IN 47403
www.iuniverse.com
1-800-Authors (1-800-288-4677)

Because of the dynamic nature of the Internet, any web addresses or links contained in this book may have changed since publication and may no longer be valid. The views expressed in this work are solely those of the author and do not necessarily reflect the views of the publisher, and the publisher hereby disclaims any responsibility for them.

Any people depicted in stock imagery provided by Thinkstock are models, and such images are being used for illustrative purposes only.
Certain stock imagery © Thinkstock.

ISBN: 978-1-4917-5993-6 (sc)
ISBN: 978-1-4917-5994-3 (e)

Library of Congress Control Number: 2015901569

Printed in the United States of America.

iUniverse rev. date: 02/06/2015

This is a biography of a man whose life was colored and transformed by the Great Depression. His actions, resulting from profound personal and economic distress, affected all around him. Names have been changed. No intent has been made to alter the truth of the characters or the events of the period. All commentaries reflecting the times are the opinions of the author.

To the Emperor, who always walked alone

Contents

About the Cover

A sunset over a Deep South cotton field is a reminder of when King Cotton was the southern mainstay. It is nostalgic in that for the true son of the South, this is the memory that helps him to remain tied to the past.

The sunset is appropriate in that it, rather than a sunrise over the same field, is symbolic because the sun has set on the old southern ways. Nothing is as the defenders of our mores intended. Progress brought with it many ills. Now the crop is picked by machine, and much lies wasted on the ground.

It is what we have lost that most concerns us, something far more precious than can be measured monetarily. And for that reason, the sunset brings the message home. The sad truth is that with the unfortunate effects of relentless progress, the South has lost its real identity.

Author's Note

Throughout this book, I have chosen to highlight with italics the four elements of the ancients: *fire, air, water*, and *earth*. As this narrative relates how my life and that of my father seemed to embrace these four ideas constantly, it seems appropriate to highlight them wherever they appear. I hope the reader will forgive this emphasis.

The Fool

The Fool stands on the precipice of
A cliff. One foot is solidly in the *air*,
Ready to complete his step. Below the ledge
Is a body of *water*, while above the Fool
A lightning bolt causes a nearby tree to
Catch *fire*. The *earth* is far below.

The Fool is presented with a question and a choice.
For guidance, he has a conversation with himself, conscious of
his subconscious, as it is necessary for important decisions.

Introduction

It was appropriate to begin this book with the Fool contemplating a leap. It would be a conscious act motivated by faith or desperation. At times I felt like the tarot fool—a card where the man (sometimes pictured as a jester) stands on a precipice with one foot on the edge and the other in the *air*. The four elements are about him in various forms. A supposed fifth element in the early classical stories was called quintessence, or aether. The latter was thought to be underlying things, perhaps spirit or soul. *Air* will suffice to contain these ideas here.

The study of tarot can be quite involved. In Jackson Square in New Orleans, tarot readings are given; however, inexperienced persons often do them. The death card appears often but like the other cards does not always indicate the obvious. And if it comes, why fear the inevitable anyway?

Fire and ice. Frost said it better than I could, but I've lived both. I've experienced the cold of bitter loneliness, the chill of a brittle north wind in my face over *water*, and the rage of a ranting maverick—a domineering father determined to mold me to his will. I searched for escape to the heavens, from which no guidance came, and to the *earth*, where it seemed a grave, my father's or my own, might be the only refuge.

The Elements and Me

My life seemed to oscillate around the four elements of the ancients. Every situation seemed to evoke one or more of them. Of course, there were reasons to rationalize concepts discussed in the time of the philosophers, long before our knowledge of the true elements and their interrelationships.

I find the idea of the four elements useful as ideas that represent repositories for our most basic emotions. For me, *fire* is useful as a symbol for hell, torment, rage, intensity, and conflict. *Air* is useful to remind me of breath, of wind, of soul, of intangibles. *Earth* suggests facts, tangibles, ends. And *water* is fluidity, current, motion, condition—stagnant or rapid, these are not elements but elementary ideas.

My life can be studied in relation to these ideas as I wandered among them and tried to find structure and meaning that could be applied to situations that arose. Most of all, *water* seems to course through these pages. I was a man drawn to *water*. In the bravest of moments and the stupidest as well, it seems that I was on or around *water*.

Near the end of my life, the elements again become a prime consideration. I will sometimes mention the Observer, who always seemed to be near me when I was on the waterways. I thought only briefly of a deity then, but now I do more often as I recall my agnostic father's eyes fixed on a ceiling at death, as if he could see through to heaven. I find myself glancing skyward as well, and I hope, as he might have, that the brief original immersion after birth was sufficient.

Yes, *water* but *fire*, *air*, and *earth* as well measured my moods, colored my thoughts, and defined me. What better partition to the compartments of life than elemental ideas? How better to separate and celebrate a life than by its phases? I was consumed by thoughts of original sin, civil rights, and the inscrutability of religion as well as the proper emphasis for desire. I became an existentialist convinced—and passionately so—of my right to freedom and belief and, as a corollary, of my obligation to the company of men and unfortunately my preference to remain aloof from them.

Throughout my life, I felt the presence of the Observer. It would be in the North on a cold duck-hunting day, in the South on a bream-fishing trip, in the East on a trip though the Virginia

Civil War battlefields, or in the West, driving through the snow geese hunting grounds of Texas or with a capricious young man on Bourbon Street in the Big Easy. I was aware of a force. This awareness may have had its source more in physics than in religion, perhaps masked in a form like kinetic energy.

It is the fall that fills me most with dread. The other seasons do not impress upon me the thought of death so quickly as the time when the goldenrod bursts into bloom, when the picked stubble of the fields still hangs draped with bits of cotton missed by the machine. I love the memory of the time when the fields were handpicked by darkies and their chilluns. I love the meadows interrupted by ragweed, goldenrod, sumac, and kudzu, and the taming of the green in the foliage. On the roadways, the cattails and black-eyed Susans still remind me of the days when Al Jolson sang in blackface.

I tried to understand life beyond the major purpose of procreation. Nothing seemed germane or universal. My study of philosophy offered little guidance, but existentialism offered some comfort. It brought me to my central planks of individual freedom and responsibility. Yet it did little to help me rationalize behavior nor did it help me to understand the many moods and outbursts of my father.

Religion only confused me. It offered no real clue to his actions. I did study various religions and belief systems, and I found reason in Buddha's ideas of impermanence and interdependence as cornerstones. He thought that all is impermanent—even the sun and Earth will die—and that all is interdependent. For instance, the tombstone that sits upright depends on the sod for its support, man upon his carbon base, the Earth upon the light of the sun, and heaven or hell on our belief systems. Perhaps like the tarot card fool, we are upon a thought precipice, about to take a leap of faith or frustration.

If philosophy and religion (as splintered into various and sometimes warring factions as it is) leave us still in search mode, can science be illuminating? Science did clarify the situation for me. It is clear that we operate on a macro (classical physics) and a micro (quantum physics) level. Now, I can appreciate how science and religion can coexist with philosophy. At last, after extensive testing, we claim to have found the Higgs boson—the so-called God particle—yet that does not mean we have found God. Rejoice, I say, as the discovery leads us into string theory and M-theory as paths to a possible and so-called Theory of Everything. Perhaps then God will be more visible to all. If not, then I fear for us.

The Beginning of the Decline

Dad's hell began in 1929. This is 2014. I have, as many in this country have, lost respect for our elected leaders. We are near a new Cold War with Russia. We remain engaged in so-called police actions around the globe, and we could become involved in defending Japan, Malaysia, or Vietnam in the South China Sea and surrounds. Worse yet, there are drones everywhere above us, rumbling about like bumblebees.

Privacy, forgive me, is a frigging joke. I am forlorn. How did we elect this misguided bunch of bickering puppets—or jockeys? Near the end of my life, I am at times filled with angst, disgust, and some abandonment of pride. It wears away daily. I wonder how a country once revered for leadership, might, and of course right could wallow in confusion over a simple job description.

Justice, what the hell is that? Children (aliens) pour over our borders daily by the thousands and expect to receive humane treatment. Recently, a bunch of freeloaders gathered in front of the White House and demanded their rights. Noncitizen lawbreakers in front of the people's home demand something they have no right to have. It makes me sick. If children can cross so easily, so can terrorists and other undesirables. Failure to secure our borders is only one of many examples of a country held hostage by the Miranda rule.

I suppose it is the abruptness of change or the inevitability of it that causes me to shudder in the realization that, with the wilting of the season, I am closing in on the confrontation with the grinning, hooded skeleton dressed in black, the scythe man, who extends a long bony finger in a beckoning gesture—an invitation to the dance macabre. As the multicolored leaves fall to carpet the *earth*, I will go unafraid but hesitant, and in all those last moments, I will wonder if life is not much more than a cruel joke.

It is appropriate that I have lived in the immediate shadow of death for the last fifteen years and have defied the odds more than once. All our southern men seem to have the indomitable will to survive. We are a tough breed, more than a little headstrong, occasionally egocentric, but there was one of us who became the epitome of all these traits: my father. This is my father's story. It is a tale told of the degradation of a personality—a sad story brought to boil by the economic calamity of the century.

Earth

1

If some alien lands after Armageddon
And sees the dry, bleached, bones of man
That litter the arid plain, *Earth* will
Mean no more to him than it did to us.

THE BURIAL

Dad never talked much about his father, but he did tell about his burial. Granddad had died sitting in a chair as he waited for a phone call from the railroad. No call came, as it was the Depression, and the rail traffic had slowed. It had always been a freight-hauling business, and with local and international trade at a standstill, most of the rail cars were idle or in receivership.

He told me that granddad's body was placed on three chairs in the parlor. He was dressed in his work overalls. Railroad men came to pay their respects during the day. In the evening, some men came and motioned Grandmother aside. My father watched as she and the two girls left the room. One of the men came to Dad and said, "We got men's business to do now, boy. You had better come with us."

Dad told me that they loaded his father into the bed of a horse-drawn wagon and motioned for Dad to get in and sit next to his father. He and a railroad man sat on either side of Granddad and

1

said nothing as they drove to a field near the railroad bed. A grave had already been dug.

Granddad was lowered into the grave. One of the men said, "These are hard times, son. We got no money for a box. He don't need it no-how. Frank was a good friend." Dad winced as the men began to shovel dirt over his dad.

One of the men turned to Dad and said, "Hard to see, boy, but got to be done. Your job is even harder. Now you got to be the man and take care of your womenfolk. Goddamned Depression hurt us all."

Another railroad man spoke up. "Sorry we couldn't get a box or a headstone. We'll try and get the stone later. You got anything to say, son?"

Strangely, Dad felt no remorse. His father had been weak, and now he had left them in a bad way, and his hopes for himself had been crushed. He knew that those railroad men would be watching him to see if he was man enough to take care of his mother and sisters.

"Well, little man, you got anything to add? You lost a father. We lost a good buddy. Don't you want to tell him good-bye? Seems like you ought to say something." Dad thought for a moment and then said, "I will never be poor again."

North Wind

In the days when I ventured out into the marshes and bays alone, I felt the presence of the Observer more than at any other time. The north wind was a brittle breath, and many a duck hunter like me felt that chill. The time in Lake Texoma, Texas, when I turned the boat over on top of me was such a time. The cold dulled my senses, yet I felt a presence. That and nothing more! I was drowning in the wash of a wave that I had foolishly created. Another camouflaged hunter saved me from death by drowning. He was a long way from me, yet he came, and by the time he got to me, I had hypothermia. A couple of minutes more, and it would have been too late.

The north wind drives the *water* out of the bays and leaves the muck visible. It is slimly and stinks. Earth is in severe distress. God, what we have done to Gaia? Long ago, an Indian would have thought nothing about drinking from a fast-moving creek. Now that it is polluted and filled with trash and debris, I wonder who would. I remember the sight of Iron Eyes Cody, an American actor, on Earth Day in 1970. Cody had a tear in his eye as he looked down from his horse onto a cluttered stream. In my youth, I did drink from a stream in the forest. Now I would not think of it.

True it is that the *air* and *water* have become our enemies. There is nothing in nature left unspoiled. There are garbage dumps in the ocean; at least one is as big as the state of Texas—a floating mass of pollutants. Much of the trash is awash from the tsunami of a few years ago. And there are dead zones at the mouths of rivers, algae blooms in municipal *water* supplies, and intensifying and frequent natural disasters. Polar bears and walruses are stranded and dying, because the ice floes that they depend on are melting. Glaciers are receding at an alarming rate. Long ago, in another book, I wrote that man in his creation of waste has brought about the fifth horseman. He should be as feared as the others. Waste, I proclaim, is the fifth and worst of the horseman.

All my years, I loved the duck hunt, enjoying the feeling of conquest against great odds. It was a Stone Age archetypal behavior for me. In the caress of the north wind, I was at my greatest. I taught my sons to brave it, to understand that a bitter chill brings out the best in us. Our reward at the end of the hunt was a hot biscuit from Hardee's.

THE EMPEROR

My father once told me that I was not successful. His definition of success was narrow. Money! As a child, my nickname for him was Daddy Scrooge. Like Scrooge, he was always counting his money and writing in his ledgers. Later, in my adulthood, I called him the Emperor, as he was always in control and vectored toward a single, all-consuming need to store up resources against another horrid depression. I think that the happiest I ever saw him was when he saw a quarter on Perdido Beach. He kept repeating, "Found money, son, the very best kind."

Dad was getting worse. He would lash out at anyone for the smallest cause. Near his horrid end, I was trying to interest him in a novel I had written, entitled *Existential Ramblings of a Southern Individualist*. I thought he might appreciate the fact that I had written and published my own book. Our conversation went like this:

"Dad, I have written a book."

"What about?"

"Mythology and its influence on religion."

"I don't read that crap. I read accounting books. You are not very successful."

"What do you mean?"

"You don't have much money and no job."

"Hell, I'm retired and disabled."

"Bullshit. You're a damn piker."

"I was a successful manager, a million-dollar salesman, and author, and a damn stockbroker. And I have two degrees."

"You never learned that accomplishments mean more than money."

"Horseshit! At least you can agree the MBA is great. You don't want to read my book."

"No, fantasy don't pay."

"Tell that to the *Harry Potter* author. She is richer now than the Queen of England."

"Well, you ain't. Get the hell out of here."

He grew up in a railroad community. My grandparents were L & N folk. Most of my ancestors on his side are buried in a little country churchyard. Their tombstones are adorned with lanterns and railroad motifs and quotes. One of my uncles was run over by the railroad, and he is in the row above my grandfather. He may have been a suicide during the Depression. I don't know for sure. A lot of the graves indicate early childhood deaths, and there are a few scattered Confederate gravesites complete with the CSA markings. It is a pretty little cemetery with wisteria, dogwood, and azaleas. I am reminded of the words of Thomas Gray in his "Elegy in a County Churchyard." Indeed, "the paths of glory lead but to the grave."

Dad had two sisters. Both were younger and looked up to him. Money was very tight during and after the Depression. He had planned to be a doctor, but had to abandon that goal to help his mother and sisters after his dad died. He worked days, nights, and weekends and managed to graduate from college. At night he caught crabs and sold them the next day if he could find a buyer; otherwise, they ate them for dinner. He also boxed in the alleyways; he got pretty good at fighting. The Depression wreaked havoc on his personality, and he resented having to take care of his womenfolk. He treated women with some contempt for all of his life.

Dad had a drawer in the family chest of drawers. One day my aunt June looked in his drawer and found some pieces of gum. She took two. When he came home and found them gone, he chased her down the street and admonished her never to go into his drawer again.

COUNTRY CEMETERY

I can imagine—don't want to, but can—the burned and trampled stubble that marked the once abundant cotton and cornfields of the South in the aftermath of the Civil War. I wasn't there, but I read about what the free blacks, the carpetbaggers, and the scalawags did to our land. I suspect that one grave near the dirt road belongs to a boy cousin of mine who died in the war at eighteen.

My great-great-grandmother and her husband lie there. She filed for a Confederate pension when my hero ancestor died. Bless him. My boys and I went to north Georgia to see his grave at Rome. He was wounded at Chickamauga. This area elicits vague sensations for me, perhaps because of the stories that my father told me of the area around Murder Creek.

THE WOOD CARVING

Dad hunted and fished at Murder Creek with his grandfather on his mother's side. He loved to squirrel hunt in the bottoms along the creek. He never said anything bad about this grandfather. Once he took me to his uncle Don and aunt Jenifer's house to spend the night. I would be sleeping when he and Don went out to hunt at daybreak.

Before bed, I needed to go to the bathroom. I had never seen an outhouse but was told that it was at the end of the path outside the kitchen door. It was dark and I was scared. At nine, it isn't hard to imagine ghosts. Above the door was a carved half-moon, and to this day I am not sure what it meant. The carving is an old southern standard.

Three times in my life, I have been a pallbearer. Once was for the last Confederate soldier, whose remains were found off Cherbourg, France, in the *USS Alabama*. I was a pallbearer for only a short distance, from the church to the hearse; other pallbearers accompanied him on a two-mile walk to the cemetery. The second time was for the wife of my brother-in-law, and the first time was for my grandmother. I was so choked up that I almost dropped her. The coffin dipped a bit, but others caught it up. Death just pisses me off. I don't know any better way to describe how I feel.

A GROWING AWARENESS

God knows I love my South. I joined the Sons of Confederate Veterans because I felt that the South should be preserved at least in memory, insofar as its charm and legacy can be saved. Now I can understand the negative ramifications of progress that the twelve prescient southerners wrote about in their book *I'll Take My Stand*. God save Dixie!

In the beginning, nothing was amiss. Civil rights were not mentioned very much. We lived on Kentucky Street until I was five. An old colored woman named Rosie came by every day, tipped her hat, and said, "Morning, Master Perry. How you been?" I'd go on playing, and she'd continue up the street to a house where she was the cleaning lady. My dad told me to say nothing to her. Back then I did what I was told to do.

Later I saw Dad really incensed against blacks. We were on vacation and were driving over the Selma Bridge when he saw a blonde woman on the arm of a black man. Dad started screaming and raising hell. My mom had a hard time with him. He was going to get out and fight the black man. Bloody Bridge, it was later called, after Reverend King marched over. Dad lived to see Obama in the White House, but we didn't speak much, so I really don't know what he said, but I can imagine his rage.

I understand the desire for equality, but I don't like the way it is perceived by some. I dislike Ebonics, for I feel that it corrupts our American language. I just react to anything that is force-fed to me. My son reminded me that skin color is not a disability. Perhaps it isn't, but willing ignorance of the customs, beliefs, and heritage of your country is, especially if it is an adopted home.

I do not accept the idea of hyphenated Americans. One is either an African or an American, an Italian or an American, a Chinese person or an American. I am to the point where I chose to be a southerner as opposed to an American because I no longer know what an American should be. I suppose if I had to be hyphenated in name, I would be a Confederate-American.

To my critics I say that loving the South does not necessarily mean hating anyone. It is an ideal that I love. The South now is as brown and effete as cotton or corn stubble. It is not and never shall be as it was. I love my memories of Uncle Remus as a kindly, smart, old black gentleman, of the Br'er Rabbit friends of mine, of Scarlet and Rhett, even of old Uncle Wiggly. I want to remember them as they were with me in my formative years.

I joined the SCV just to be counted, simply to let my membership offset some ethnic or antigun rights group. This was not for spite or a throwback to a browned ideal, but simply to express the idea that the simple majority of white folks are still proud of their history. It seems strange that whites are perceived to have fallen demographically into a lower status. It is our fault, and it is because we were and are complacent. We ignored our obligation to our ancestors. Now the Confederacy is just a footnote.

For me, race was never the problem. I could care less if a man was purple or polka dotted. My objection was and is attitude. Payback for wrongs, the idea that I stand accused by some ancestral omission, is similar in a way to the idea of original sin: I am stained by an ancient wrong. I have always believed that a man should apologize for his own sins and not for those he inherits. I watched the world change, and truly my South is lost to me. I don't recognize it, and I miss old black Rosie, who always asked, "How you been, Master Perry?" when she passed. I too long for equality, and I wonder if my race may have to wait a while for its realization.

RELATIVES

Mother had five sisters and three brothers. I was close to two of the sisters. One of them had a small bar where my cousins and I would sit and listen to country music while our parents had a suds or two. I loved to listen to Hank Snow and Roy Acuff; "The Great Speckled Bird" was my favorite gospel piece. I had an uncle who fished all the time in the Yellow River near Milton, Florida, but I met him only once or twice, and my other uncle was killed in a kamikaze strike off Okinawa.

Dad ruined these associations for me; he did work for the family and treated them so badly that they had nothing to do with us. It hurt my mother. They were great fishermen, and I would have learned much from them. My cousin Denny and I were close buddies for a while. Denny never married, and many years later he died of a strange kind of pneumonia.

I dearly loved my aunt Nancy. She always had presents for me at Christmas. My father never liked holidays or birthdays and didn't give anyone any gifts. However, he never refused to receive. I had to try to explain to my young children why their grandfather never gave them anything. In college, I got into trouble, and I knew Dad would not help me, so I called Aunt Nancy, and she sent me the money to pay off my poker debt. I paid her back and also learned to fold occasionally.

My father was rough on my aunt, and she constantly gave him hell for the way he treated my mother. He treated all women with contempt. He thought women existed only to serve men. I never doubted that he loved my mother and his grandchildren, but outwardly he was not capable of demonstrating love.

THE DEPRESSION

To me, the Depression was kind of like taking the movies *Gone with the Wind*, *Song of the South*, and the *Grapes of Wrath* and editing them into one. The pictures taken of the Dust Bowl folk—the women whose faces perfected angst and despair—are the images burned into my mind. And Scarlet on a burned plantation field, swearing that she would survive. And Uncle Remus happy, proud, and content to be as God made him. The blacks don't like the idea of a slave on a plantation, even in a movie, yet if they really paid attention, it is apparent that Uncle Remus was a loved and respected man. Again, this is about attitude. These are three different movies suggesting hard times and resilient folk, in contrast to Br'er Rabbit and friends, who brought laughter onto the scene.

Dad told of the day that he hitched a ride to New Orleans to find his father, who at that time was employed for a few days. He said that my grandfather bought him the finest dinner he ever had. Then he stowed away on a railroad car for the return trip. Dad said that he could relate to those in hobo camps and railcars, because more than once he got a ladle of onion soup from someone who had little too give.

He learned to sue people and control them. He could charm anyone into doing things for him, but seldom did he reciprocate.

I think that he felt he had been dealt a bad hand in life and his goal justified any behavior and any means.

He was horrid to my dear aunt Penny, who suffered for years with debilitating back pain. She was in a hospice for years, and he never went to see her. I had to go and tell him that she had died.

"Dad, I got bad news," I said.

"What other kind is there?"

"Aunt Penny has died. I'm sorry."

"When?"

"Today Aunt June called and asked me to come over and tell you. I'll take you to the airport."

"What the hell for?"

"So you can go to the funeral."

"Costs too much. Won't do her no good."

"Give me some money. I'll send flowers."

"Get the hell out of here. Leave me alone."

The Threat

Finally I could not stand his treatment of my mother any longer, and I confronted him, saying, "I think Mother is unhappy."

"Why?"

"She wears old clothes. You don't give her anything. Aunt Nancy has reservations about how you treat her."

"That bitch is a thorn in my side. Anyway, who the hell are you to talk to me like that?"

"I'm her son, and I got a right to talk for her."

"Well, buster boy, I don't like it. Shut up."

"I won't, and you can't make me."

"The hell I can't. I gave you life, and I can damn well take it away."

I could not believe that he had actually implied that he would kill me. It wasn't the last time I would be stunned by his words. There was *fire* in his eyes that day and on many more to come.

GOLF BALLS

I estimate two thousand golf balls in the closets, garage, and foyer at my dad's two properties. Dad loved to collect balls. He did it with an eye to eventual sale but also for the joy of collecting. He would walk the course each day and pick up those that had been abandoned in the rough.

One day I was with him when a twosome teed off. We watched as the ball bounced to the edge of the rough. "Close enough," said Dad as he picked it up. We watched as the two golfers in the distance looked in vain for the ball they knew should have been there.

This went on for forty years or more. As a boy, I went with him to walk the course near Gulf Shores. He said, "Rich men play here. Get some Titlist balls, I 'spect." He would find a ball and toss it to me to put in my pocket. In the end, the balls didn't sell, and I gave them all to charity. It was fun to walk the course with him as a boy. I only wish I could have done it once more.

GUN SAFETY

When I was ten, I thought my dad was wise, fair, and deserving of respect. He and I were busy remodeling the old family home in Oakdale in Mobile, Alabama. Much needed to be done with the floors, the roof, and the sewer system. I hated working on the house, especially rodding out the sewer line and varnishing the floors. Dad paid me three dollars a day, but he insisted that I put the money into savings bonds. I never had any spending money of my own.

During those days, Dad told me about how my grandfather was in the backyard and a flock of crows landed in the oak tree. He got his single-shot, sixteen-gauge shotgun and waited for them to bunch up. He rested the barrel of the gun on his boot, and it slipped off into the mud. When he shot at the crows, it blew the end of the barrel off, and it knocked him down. Dad laughed and got a whipping for it.

That was the house that I lived in until I was five years old. It was a two-bedroom, one-bath house with a small front parlor. Two large oak trees were in the backyard; one of them grew into the side of the house. Honeybees made a nest in a crack, and we had them flying around inside the house for a while. The oaks did help the soil, and we had lots of fat earthworms for bait.

A Perspective of the Times

I guess in those days I became aware that something had changed significantly. Sometimes I remembered old black Rosie, who would pass me and say, "How you been, Master Perry?" One day, a black man passed by, and I asked about old Rosie. He said, "She ded." It was the way he told me—sharp, sarcastic, without a measure of respect. On reflection, at that moment I became a part of the civil rights situation; I realized that we were different from blacks in more than just color.

In truth, the civil rights movement had its taproot in the warm bowels of the South. It was cotton and the intense hands-on farming of it (with the North being the avaricious main consumer) that necessitated conflict. Agrarian practices were too slow. The picture of darkies dragging their pregnant croaker sacks down the long rows of cotton was simply too much for northern folk to bear. To them, it was obvious that mechanization was overdue. Later *Uncle Tom's Cabin* came out in print, and Lincoln was convinced of his might-makes-right solution.

Yes, the southern taproot goes further back than I can remember. President Theodore Roosevelt invited Booker T. Washington from Tuskegee, Alabama, to dine with him in the White House. It was the first such overture by an American president to a black person.

For the rest of my life, the civil rights involvement became a sad focal point of my experience—a timeline to mark the phases of my life. I had encounters with blacks, and once was cut up pretty badly by four of them. They caught me alone one night and cut me with broken beer bottles. Dad hated them and used the N word often. It was their attitude that bothered me most, as if I were in some measure responsible for their plight.

The neighborhood where we lived quickly changed. Dad told me that many of the white folks were selling their homes and moving away. He said that was the reason we were fixing up the old homestead. A lot of blacks had moved into the area, and the park at the end of the street had only blacks. White kids didn't go to the pool anymore; it was too dangerous.

I think back on the comment "She ded." He might as well have said, "Your South is dead." In essence, that is what happened. My wife-to-be lived only a few streets away, but her family had to move to a trailer for their safety. The only sensible defense against inclusion was to leave.

My wife and brother-in-law tell stories of what it was like to live there before the exodus and what it was like to be a child playing in the KC ditch and catching catfish and going to the Roosevelt Theater, where for fifteen cents you could watch a double feature, a cartoon, a serial, and some news. The Cotton Patch was nearby, and if you had enough money, you could get a hamburger.

I am probably in the last two years of my life. I never thought that I would live with a black mayor, a black president, and black judges and congressmen, but the fellow who sneered and said, "She ded," was right. The South that I knew and loved had died an agonizingly slow but complete death. I can remember the forester's comment about what it meant to be a southerner: "Most important, son—the meaning behind Tara's theme."

Naturally, I am proud to be among one of the few remaining true southern sons. My heritage is one of my most prized possessions.

THE ALLEYWAY FIGHTS

I asked Dad about the alleyway fights. Men would gather in a circle in some out-of-the-way alley, and the combatants would fight until one of them could not continue. Dad said that it was common in the Depression and that good fighters even traveled from city to city. I wanted to know about his last fight. He told me the following:

"It happened one afternoon near the bakery on Broad Street. Prize was five dollars. All went to the winner."

"Doesn't seem like a lot to fight for."

"Lot of fights before that last one. *Earth* is a hard canvas, boy. You can break ribs on a fall."

"I wouldn't fight for five dollars."

"Then five dollars would buy fresh bread and a piece of meat. Not hard, crusted, stale bread, but fresh."

"What happened?"

"I had to fight a stevedore. Steel man, brute, a mountain of flesh. I was outweighed at least fifty pounds."

"Don't seem fair."

"Wasn't supposed to be. Fight was bare chested, bare knuckles. No quarter, no rules. Way it was, then."

Dad went on to tell how the big man knocked him down twice. He figured he was a goner unless he could outsmart the fellow, and that is what he did. Dad pretended to go down on one knee after he let the guy graze him. Then, as the man bent down to finish him off, Dad lunged at him.

"He was a brutal bastard. I knew he'd make a show of me. I hit him square in the eye with all I had. He screamed and fell to the ground. I jumped on him and broke his nose. Then I knocked him out with a kick to his jaw."

"That was dirty."

"It was war. I got my money. Fresh bread! God knows It had been a while since we had any. Leader gave me the money and told me to get the hell out of there and never fight again. He said, the stevedore man and his friends would put the word out. Next time, I'd die."

Then he said that he ran home and gave his mother $4.50. I asked, "You kept fifty cents?" His answer was that he had earned it.

Dad quit the fights and got into catching crabs at night and selling them during the day. On days when nobody would buy, they would eat them for dinner. Soft-shell season was best, and he could save a buck or two in his private drawer. He would have kept it all, but he knew that the railroad men were watching him. Another time he told me, "Boy, when you have to fight, don't fart around. Hit and hit hard. Ain't no ethics in war. If your damn enemy sees you indecisive, you will pay dear. I promise you."

DEATH

Death is never simple. The mechanical process of reviews and the tabulation of assets and their disposition instantly colors the fact of the passage. Not euphemistically, Dad crossed over, but an avalanche of problems accompanies the reality of a passing.

And one asset subject to quick dissolution is love. I was surprised by one relative indifferent to all but what she might receive. I felt and still feel complete repugnance for her. Most family relationships are earthy in nature—that is, basic and primal.

Dad and I could have been great together. Both of us had huge egos that would never permit reconciliation—only a grudging respect for each other. One should love his father, but as my son Tom said, it was a "tough love," and it left horrid scars on both of us.

Dad told me of his hatred of sweet potatoes—yams to most folks. In the Depression, they were about the only food that the family had after Dad's father died. He said they poured molasses on the yams and garnished them with wild onions. The sight of yams made him sad, as he thought of how hard my grandmother worked in her garden. She had a college degree, and before the Depression she had taught school.

As a gardener, I loved the feel of soil in my hands. Now that I think on it, I can champion the ancient idea of it as mother: corn mother to the Meso-Americans. You plant the seed, and if it's nurtured, it bursts out of the *earth* and takes its measure of responsibility. At death, it seems natural to expect to be returned to the *earth*.

Dad died with no wish for the soil. He feared decomposition. One day we had this conversation:

"Dad, when you die, where do you want to be buried?"

"Nowhere, I don't want to rot like damn roadkill with maggots feasting on me."

"What then, cremation?"

"Hell no, I'll burn soon enough. Postpone it as I can."

Later we found out he wanted his body given to a medical school. No closure, no obituary, nothing to say to a public he detested anyway. He died last in his college class. I would never have guessed that the man who never gave gifts to his children or grandchildren would give the world the gift of himself.

I can't wrap my arms around his death. I never saw him at rest in a casket overlaid with flowers. Worse, I feel comfortable with the *earth*—a place for me to visit, to apologize. Now there is nothing. I picked up his ashes from the medical school when they were done carving him, and I carried my father under my arm in a simple tin. Finally, I disposed of his ashes in a manner that would have pleased him. Sad, I needed to bury the total seed, not just the chaff. Gardeners like God and my grandmother would understand.

Yet why should I regret the lack of a grave? It matters not for any of us. The earth is but a temporary container. Science tells us that our planet will be destroyed by red-giant decay or asteroid death, most probably before the collision of the Milky Way and the Andromeda galaxy, but even before that, all traces of man will be gone. *Earth* will be splintered or vaporized, and all the graves will be spilled into space.

Water

I see the *water* as a mirror
For my tempestuous soul.
My moods are reflected and
Enhanced by the realization of my
Near-death experiences in its depths

NEARER, MY GOD, TO THEE

I see *water*. Rolling waves, a rocking boat, dense fog over the Tensaw River that shrouds the World War II ghost fleet that once was anchored there. Surplus remnants of a war—all were sold for scrap or to Third World nations or made into fishing reefs.

The *water* closes over me. I have been a careless hunter. My hip waders fill and pull me down toward the dark, cold depths below. It is a brittle day in late January on Brushy Creek in Lake Texoma, Texas. I see a red gas can floating way above me as well as decoys, two dead greenhead mallards, and assorted gear. I am confused but think to cut my hip waders loose from the belt loops. Hypothermia is beginning to caress me as I fight back to the surface, where I am finally rescued by the only other hunter out that day.

Thirty-nine years later I am again thrashing about in the *water* on Blakely River near Spanish Fort, Alabama, and my obesity

17

prevents me from being pulled into the skiff. I am towed to shore as I cling to the small boat. I am black and blue all over but alive, thanks to Wesley, my brother-in-law.

I see an uncle fishing in the Yellow River near Milton, Florida. He drops his bream pole and reaches for his pocketknife. Uncle Chris grasps the moccasin behind the head and slices through his pants leg. Then he cuts the snake's head off and watches as the carcass sinks into the brackish *water*. He is unperturbed and continues to fish.

Fishing

The best times I had with my father were when we went bream fishing. It was about an hour and a half to the Tensaw River, one of the five rivers that empty into my beloved Mobile Delta. On the way, we would listen to Slim Whitman sing "Rose Marie." Whitman's voice relaxed us both.

Our destination was what was once called Nigger Lake. Later it was changed to Negro Lake for political correctness. I think it may have been changed again. In my mind, the place will always have the name I remember. A railroad trestle crossed over the river to the entrance to the lake. Sometimes the fog would roll in over the river and make the crossing extra dangerous.

Off of the lake proper were a number of bayous, including Oak and Smith's. Smith's was my favorite. It was lined all along the banks with grass and lily pads, and in the spring the edges and the woods were all shades of green. Dad would skull the boat along with a long oar out of the back of the transom. We would drop fish as we moved. Dad kept even the small bream. "Protein, buster boy, protein. He'll fry up good."

I loved this kind of fishing. I longed to see the red cork slip below the water, loved to watch as a fat goggle-eye or a large bluegill or shellcracker came to the net. Dad had a trailer up on the high bluff at the landing. We would stay there over the weekend.

Occasionally, Aunt Nancy and Cousin Denny would come. Usually, by the end of the second day, they would be fighting.

THE EMPEROR

My father had no tolerance for criticism, and Aunt Nancy was quick to remind him of the way he treated my mother. I came to call him the Emperor in those days. His drinking made it all the worse. You could not look long into the Emperor's eyes, as they would hold you spellbound. He reminded me of a picture of the mad Russian mystic, Rasputin; his fiery eyes seemed to be the whole of him.

The Emperor was six feet tall with black, wavy hair in those days. He walked ramrod straight and loved to run along the fairways of the golf course. He was not a member, but to him that was no matter. His clothes were always out of style. New ones, if any, came from Goodwill. Dad wore plaid sport coats in the nineties that he had worn in the forties. Long after men quit wearing suspenders, Dad could be seen in old red ones. Thin ties came in, but he always wore the same wide ones that he wore in his college days. In short, he was, as I became later, an anachronistic, iconoclastic, southern individualist whose twin passions were the quest for money and fishing for bream. Simply stated, he was not a man to care about convention or fashion.

We shared a love of the delta. The incredible flora and fauna—the hoary hair of Spanish moss, the jagged cypress knees, the *water* hyacinths that sheltered the green trout and the fat goggle-eye, the squeal of a wood duck in flight, the osprey nest in the tall dead tree or atop a telephone pole, the bellow of an alligator—all this we shared around every bend of Oak and Smith's bayous.

He was a numbers man; he always has figures in his head as to his net worth. By trade he was an accountant—the ultimate Dr. Jekyll and Mr. Hyde type. One minute he was the perfect charmer, and the next he became an absolute tyrant. Many times, I saw that aspect of him while fishing, especially when I was seven or eight. We fished Fish River long before the developers made an asphalt jungle of its banks. Dad often said, "Who the hell wants to fish near a backyard or at the end of the eighteenth hole." So we found remote places to fish. Both of us came to hate developers for their rape of the land.

We even put a trailer on a bank we called KBC Point, which reflected my kids' first names. It was on a creek in a little town that had been settled by German immigrants. It was famous for the local sausages.

Scotty

I had a little Scottie dog that I loved, and we would take him fishing. One day I didn't see my dog in our boat and I looked around and saw him floating on a log in the middle of the Tensaw River. He had climbed onto the log as it floated by us. I screamed at my father to get him, but Dad did nothing, so I pulled up the anchor. He was mad at me, because we were catching a lot of bream. We got Scotty, but Dad would have let him die. He was unfeeling, uncaring, and entirely absorbed in himself and his wants. No one else mattered, and from that point on, I was fully aware of that.

Scotty was my constant companion, my confidant, my only buddy. Dad was never close to the dog. I think Scotty knew better than to get close to him. We had other animals, but all had unfortunate and untimely ends, such as King and Queen. They were a pair of bluetick coonhound puppies that Dad had been given by a client. He would not pay for any veterinarian bills, and both soon died of distemper. I also had a pet hamster that got sick. Dad made me kill it.

The Emperor was the absolute authority in all things, a despotic ruler, unprincipled, materialistic—at times, a mean man worse than any I ever read about in literature. Worse, I imagine, than old Huck Finn's dad. Control was his only aim. He had to hold tight reins on everyone, including Mom and me.

THE DEPRESSION SICKNESS

He described the Depression as a time of turmoil, sadness, disbelief, trepidation, and tribulation. It was a period that saw the rise of plagues, locusts, jackrabbits, and lizards in the Midwest and the rise of gangsters like Dillinger and Bonnie and Clyde, who became folk heroes because of their war on the banks. It was also a time that saw the reality of bread lines, camps, and suicides. It seemed like a prelude to Armageddon.

Men prayed less, and what they prayed for wasn't salvation but necessities like food, shelter, and rain. If they prayed at all, it was more for their bodies than their souls. The word *entitlement* wasn't much in use; Social Security and food stamps were yet to come. I remember my conversation with Dad's about praying during the Depression:

"Dad, I know it was a horrid time. You musta prayed a lot."

"Why the hell you ask me that? You know I don't believe in that fairy tale."

"What fairy tale?"

"Heaven. A place of happiness and joy. No such place."

"You sure?"

"Hell yes! I tell you this for certain. If there was a second coming, God I say, if God is, then he has already sent our savior."

"I don't think Jesus is due yet."

"Not him, nitwit."

"Who then?"

"Franklin Delano Roosevelt. I cried the day he died, and that is one of the only two times I ever have cried."

I asked him about the other time, but he didn't answer. I imagine it was when his first child died. He went on to talk of the Depression in Mobile and the Dust Bowl out West. That interests me, because now I have a lung ailment like what many of them

21

had; I am dying of fibrosis in the lungs. There the soil darkened the sky, and pieces of sand shredded lungs as surely as would a scalpel.

THE RAILROAD

The L & N was part of the southern railway system. When I was about twelve, I rode the Hummingbird by myself to Dayton, Ohio. I went there to spend time with Uncle Redd. No man ever had a better uncle. He was fun and never mad, and he was one of the only two friends my father ever had. The other was a renowned local bandleader who taught me piano for a year.

I remember the speed of the train. How the countryside just seemed to fly by me! It was the fastest that I had ever gone. In those days, you could see deer by the tracks and, if you were real lucky, perhaps even a black bear. Bears are almost gone now in Alabama, and that is a damn shame.

The second memory I have was when the train crashed into Big Bayou Canot in 1993. I knew one of the engineers onboard. A barge got loose in the fog and rammed the bridge supports. When the Sunset Limited train crossed, it jumped the tracks and careened into the bayou. The cab was almost totally mired in the mud. My friend died in that morass. The train crashed only a little ways from my duck blind in Little Catfish Bayou. Had I been fishing or duck hunting that day, would I have tried to rescue someone? I like to think that I would have, as I was twice rescued later.

I have been saddened to notice that good deeds on the *water*, while expected if in trouble, are not always forthcoming. Twice I was stranded and I flagged down someone to help. Once the man said he would help me when he got through fishing, and he sped off. The next said he would turn his boat around to better position the tow, and he sped off. I was with Ginny once in a storm with lightning and heavy rain. I was worried about Ginny but went to get an old man and his son. They had flagged me down in that bad storm. What the hell. The times they are a'changing.

The railroad comes to mind when I think of the Civil War and my great-great-granddad's effort. The rail hub at Corinth, Mississippi, was too much of a prize for the federals to ignore. The capture of the Mobile & Ohio Railroad would hasten the end of the war. The battle at Shiloh was horrid, and the dead were covered in peach blossoms. This was a war we were obliged to fight for honor, if for no other reason. Yes, my ancestor and his fellows fought hard. He was wounded at Chickamauga.

The railroad archetype courses through me and through the blood of my children. One of their grandfathers, two of their great-grandfathers, and many of their ancestor, uncles, and cousins were railroad folk, and I say that with pride.

GOLDENDALE

As I remember Goldendale, it was a sleepy little hamlet on the Eastern Shore of Mobile Bay. In the heart of town was a pharmacy, a hardware store, a Ford car dealership, a tax collection office, and a town newspaper. The tax system is based on an idea set out in the works of the economist Henry George. It is an arrangement where you lease the property for a long term. Dad didn't like the setup, and neither do I. Even then, Goldendale was a retirement community. At the bottom of the hill was a long, high pier where kids would go to swim. Some dove off the pier and were seriously hurt.

On the beach was a walk-in theater that was open in the summer. It was an open-air, sit-on-benches theater where one could watch the local high school gymnast perform. At eleven I watched her and had the first awareness of an unknown need. It was a clear night, and the stars were brilliant overhead.

The town has changed over the fifty years since I went to high school. It was written up in a national magazine, and land values rose. Flower boxes and plots of tulips, pansies, and petunias were everywhere, as if the town itself was the center of a bouquet. That tradition has continued. The pier is longer now and in better shape, but the little theater is gone.

THE SILENT SPRING WARNING

But this idyllic transformation came at a price. Population increased dramatically, yacht clubs sprang up, beachfront owners built piers in front of their houses that may have interrupted some of the natural *water* flow, and suddenly there was serious pollution. Occasionally, the beaches would be closed due to coliform bacteria counts. Progress, it seemed, doomed the city and its bay.

Long before I'd ever heard about fecal bacteria or low dissolved oxygen content, Dad took me down to the Goldendale pier. A lot of kids were swimming and splashing *water* on each other. I looked up at the father that I then idolized and asked him to teach me to swim. He said, "Nothing to it boy. You learn by doing. Experience is the best teacher."

With that statement, he picked me up and threw me off the lower platform. I wanted to learn, because I wanted to impress him. I floundered about as the other kids laughed. He watched but said nothing until he motioned me to climb out on the wooden ladder. On the way home, he said, "See what I mean by experience."

"No, that was a cruel thing to do."

"Well, you swam. Not well, but you did. Better learn to be on your own and not beholden to me or any other man."

BLAKELY

I almost drown in Blakely River. I hit a wave and was tossed clear of the boat and was in distress immediately from the poor condition of my lungs and my obesity. My brother-in-law, Wesley, saved me after he finally realized that I had been ejected. I never panicked.

Less than a half mile up from where I went over is mama's ditch, which is a short, landlocked creek in which we had some good memories, such as Mom and Dad and me against a bank overhung with climbers, where we would fish straight out into the creek. It was my mother's favorite place.

Blakely is one of my favorite rivers and one of the five that empty into the Mobile Delta. It holds the best memories for me. It was a sanctuary for my mother. I don't ever remember Dad being mean to her in that place, so it was special to each of us.

Not far from Mama's ditch is the old fort on the junction of the Blakeley and Apalachee Rivers. The Confederates had a position there, and the submerged pilings have destroyed many a boat that cut too close to shore. It is a prime fishing spot in November. The Confederates mined the waters with what they called torpedoes. Several Union ships were sunk. The main Fort Blakely, which is nearby, fell on April 9, 1865, and the point fort was abandoned soon after.

I think of my ancestors in that war and how they tried to preserve the idea of states' rights—that Alabama should be sovereign, with its own laws. Our culture, our belief systems, and our way of life were forever changed by that war. I lay it at the feet of that horrible idea called progress and submit that progress never has a maturity date.

THE FLOW

A life passes, and you wonder not at the achievement or the lack of it but of the flow, the movement, the flux of change. Dad lived with a goal that no one understood. It was disguised by distrust of his fellow man and a bitterness displayed toward anyone who challenged his authority.

I was all too often the subject of the Emperor's tirades, yet in retrospect there were good times. I loved to listen to *Amos and Andy* with him and Mom, and we laughed when Kingfish would happen on one of his get-rich schemes with Andy.

We fished for beam in Negro Lake and used the old bamboo fly rod to fish for channel cat around the ghost fleet, although it was illegal, and we were often chased out by patrol boats. Dad said he didn't give a damn if it was illegal or not, because they didn't own the water.

I can still see the hill with the three crosses that we always passed, a reminder of a time that was to come, a chill as we then passed the Burma Shave signs in a neat row, heard Slim Whitman singing "Rose Marie" and "Annie Laurie," and finally got our hooks in the water. These were the moments that I treasured, when the flow was warm and there was a sense of unity among us. However, as I got older, the chill returned as my dad wanted to direct my life, but only one of us could be the charioteer.

I especially loved when we seined for our own bait. We used a two-man pole net with cork floats on the top and small weights on the bottom. When I cleaned out Dad's garage, the old net crumbled in my hands, and I cried. In those days, in the *Amos and Andy* times, he and I were tight.

Yet I can't explain the guilt, the numbness, the fog in my mind. I could have been a better son, he a better father. When Mama died, I said, *"Vaya con dios,"* to her. When I last saw him, I simply said, "So long, Dad." I can't go to Mama's ditch without thinking of both of them. He didn't hear me say good-bye, as his eyes were fixed on the ceiling. Not even a blink. In the shadows, the grim reaper lurked always, in collection mode.

Never did Dad mention my dear mother, who slaved for him and me for all of her life. She did most of the bookkeeping work, and the *water* brings back the happier times that I had with her. I can't shake the feeling that I will have another momentous and final encounter with *water*. Perhaps, as it was so prominent in my life and in theirs, it is as appropriate an end as can be for me. I know that there will come a third and final drowning episode. My lungs will fail, and I will drown in my own sea of blood.

This expectation paints my melancholy. I am blue, forlorn, engaged in a primordial wonderment with life and death. Life, it seems, is a cruel joke. You become the best you can be then robustly tread toward an oblivion that can only be imagined. It is mandated by a blueprint drawn by someone named God. And there is only forward, no retreat, no pause as the next second prohibits such a possibility. It is the philosophers' simple summary statement known as the arrow of time and the physical second law of thermodynamics, which in effect says that order inevitably leads to disorder—that is, life to death. In this sense, the physical law confirms religious doctrine. So it is, and it cannot be otherwise.

UNCLE REDD

Uncle Redd had a clown's heart. He was a simple man who loved life. Redd was my mentor as a child. To be with him was grand. When I became a man, Ginny and I visited Redd and his wife, Junc, several times. We talked of Dad and masonry while we ate boiled shrimp and drank Pabst Blue Ribbon.

"Your dad is hard on you," he said during one visit.

"I know. Nothing I do pleases him."

"Then do nothing. Serve him right, eh?"

"Redd, will I ever be a success?"

"Depends on who is looking at you. If I am, yes; if he is, no. Success is a warm thing. It is contentment, a realization that you are part of a plan that will have meaning. I guess that is part of the old bricklayers' message. Build according to plan. Yep, I'm proud of you, million-dollar salesman, Master Mason, regional manager for a major company, MBA, author. Pass the Pabst. You done much, boy. Feel warm about it."

PAPER MOON

I always felt uncomfortable when I looked at the moon. I remember when the moon was full as I motored into the bays to duck hunt. In the shadow that was near and the gray that was far, there seemed to be a chilling contrast.

I envisioned unseen perils with a full moon. Of course I thought about Tranquility Base, the man in the moon's face, his pockmarked surface, as if he'd had a serious case of acne. As I would get closer to my blind, the weird figures cast by shrubs on the bank brought a strange comfort, as the enclosure was home.

The movie *Paper Moon* really solidified the idea of the Depression for me. I took Mother in her plain, faded dress with her belly tumor so prominent that it brought stares and grimaces. That is the memory I carried with me on those hunts alone in Chocalatta Bay. Yet taking Mother was the best thing I ever did, and it was only the second movie I remember her ever seeing.

All through the movie, as the bad guy fleeced the destitute, I thought of my father. How could he do what he did in such a ruthless manner—and all for the almighty dollar? To this day I remember the tune of "Paper Moon," but I don't recall if it was the Ink Spots or the Mills Brothers that made it a hit. I gave my mother a night on the town with her boy and left the miser at home with his ledgers.

The moon has always fascinated me. The sun always seems the same, but the moon changes. It can be bright yellow, brilliant orange, or even red. It seems to have a personality with changing moods, and I sense my own personality revolve through mood swings as I am under its spell on a cold winter night in the marsh. I try not to think too hard about Mother and tell myself it is only a paper moon that brings me to tears.

THE FORESTER

Dad was not a forgiving man. Not a man to allow a mistake. When he told me that we were going on a bream-squirrel float trip around the lake, I was excited. He was going to bring a forester friend and cautioned me to be still and shut up. He also said that he would allow me to shoot his .22-caliber Winchester single-shot rifle. Man, oh man, was I ever the excited eight-year-old.

"Pay attention," he told me. "This man is a client. Pays us a tidy sum. Learn from this man."

"Learn what?" I asked.

"He knows the forest. He earned a wood badge in Scouts. He is as true a southerner as you will ever know. I'll get him to tell you what it means to be a southerner."

Dad went on to tell me to get the gear ready and not to forget the tackle box. On the way to Boatyard Lake, the forester told me what it means to be a southerner, saying, "Young fella. A true southerner needs to know much about his South."

He told me about the magnolia and the dogwood; the Bonnie Blue Flag and the Confederate battle flag; buttercups, red clover, cattails, and pitcher plants; carpetbaggers, sharecroppers, kudzu, and goldenrod; Faulkner, Lanier, and Ransom; cotton and peanuts; Iron City beer, Pabst, Jax, and Bud; rabbit tobacco; possums, coons, watermelon, collard greens, and grits; Uncle Remus, Little Black Sambo, and the Br'er boys; picking blackberries, walking barefoot, and catching crawfish; and most important, the meaning behind Tara's theme.

I thanked him. We got there just before dawn as a low fog was merging with the Spanish moss hanging on the oaks. Dad and the forester put the Voyager 4.2-horsepower outboard on the skiff we rented, and we were set to go. But the motor would not start.

"Son, hand me the tackle box," Dad said. "Old baby needs new plugs."

"Sorry, Dad, I guess I forgot the tackle box."

"You stupid little shit!"

They tried to get the motor started but couldn't, so we went home.

"Don't be so hard on the boy," the forester said. "We will go again."

We never did. Dad bitched all the way home. I guess the client didn't like it, because he left Dad soon after. I got blamed for the loss. "I told you to get the damn box," he said.

"I'm sorry."

"Yes, you are 'bout as sorry as they come. Hard to believe you got my blood in you."

That tongue lashing hurt me. It hurt not to measure up. Not to be perfect when perfect was needed, like on a bream-squirrel float trip on one of the prettiest lakes in Alabama.

Now I contemplate the remainder, that part of Hamlet's soliloquy to be that comes swift like a shot—here before the contemplation of it is ended. What will I do with the remainder of my life? I will become a spectator, a dreamer. I set my sights on yesterday, when it was bouncy and gravid. I will live in the memory of Mom; Aunt Nancy, whom I dearly loved; Uncle Redd, whose cracker-box philosophy still rings true; my wife, children, and grandchildren; the others who were close to me; Dad, my antagonist, always my tormentor; and of course my southern roots. Shakespeare said, "Take arms against a sea of troubles and by opposing end them." I submit that I did my best.

Hopefully the memories will grow warmer in the same sense that absence makes the heart grow fonder. I am and will be content with my life, both the mistakes and triumphs. I remain grateful for who I am and where I have been. I took firm steps when firmness was required and emerged from the mist satisfied. I had a great partner in my wife through all those years. Finally, as an existentialist, I accept full responsibility for all my actions.

About a month after Dad's death, I went through a number of photos. Some showed a grizzled, weathered old codger who had bested every tempest thrown against him. One was of him holding up a bluegill on his bream pole. This is the memory I choose to keep: Dad, who was the fisherman, the warrior, a man like me who loved the *water*. He was happy, triumphant against the backdrop of lily pads and brackish *water*, hyacinths, and Spanish moss. Mayflies and dark green overhanging boughs were his copacetic heaven and mine.

MY UFO EXPERIENCE

I had more than my share of profound experiences on the *water*. Once I went duck hunting by myself and left the landing long before daybreak, as I liked to hear the marsh sounds at night and to smell the methane near the shore. I would light a cigar and drink coffee from my thermos. Boomer, my Labrador retriever, was with me. We parked in our blind in the first pocket of Chocalatta Bay.

I had put out my decoys, and as I was petting my dog, a light came out of the sky and illuminated my blind. It was a funnel-shaped light and appeared to retreat to a pinpoint source above. There was no refraction, no reflection, no plane—just a weird light, nothing more. It scared the hell out of me and the dog. It lasted for maybe twenty seconds and then abruptly was gone. Daylight was still a full hour away.

Later there was a sighting of a supposed UFO in Mississippi near Pascagoula, which was a distance from us that an aircraft like a UFO could have made in quick time. Two men alleged that they had been captured and released by aliens. I often wonder if a UFO was over me that day and if the aliens rejected me because of the dog or the dog because of me. The Pascagoula sighting made national news.

The Cajun Incident

Dad never gave much thought to anyone other than himself. I fault him, but I am ashamed to do so, because I truly believe that he was incapacitated. I remain convinced that he was unsettled in the mind because of the damn Depression. I remember an episode that took place in winter in a Cajun hunting camp south of Marrero, Louisiana. I was a member of that camp and had invited him to come along to fish.

The first night, after much drinking and card playing, we went to bed. Dad complained about the cold. The Cajuns told him that he could not turn on the heater because it was dangerous. A number of friends of ours had died in a nearby camp from a faulty heater. Dad kept protesting and was told to shut up.

Later that night, when we were all asleep, he got up and lit the heater. The Cajuns were furious, and I was told to take him home and to never bring him back. We left, and on the way back to the landing I pulled over to the creek bank. I stopped the boat and asked him. "Why the hell did you do it?"

"I was cold."

"You endangered all our lives."

"I don't give a fuck about them."

"You were their guest."

"I was cold. Figured one of us would get up."

"You could have killed us. It was dumb."

"I was cold. Now drive the damn boat."

The fact that his action could have killed me was not the cause of my anger. He had embarrassed me in front of my Cajun friends. I had to resign from the camp.

THE DELTA

I loved the Mobile Delta, that large tract of tidal land, swamp, and estuaries around Mobile Bay. There I fished and hunted all my life, and it was there that I introduced my two sons to a love of nature and taught them to hunt and fish, to recognize danger, to shiver in the cold without complaint, to appreciate the hunt itself more than the kill, to be as grateful for an empty stringer as for a full one—in short, to be men. For me, to be in the delta with its myriad flora and fauna was a privilege. I wrote a book, *The Front Pew,* about the boys and me hunting together there.

Yet I was forced to watch as condos began to appear, as civilization encroached on the edges and polluted the pristine environment. As late as 2009, great blue herons, egrets, rails, ducks, and fish were dying in pools of oil left by seemingly unconcerned oil companies. I cursed as I saw the banks of Bateau Bay littered with paper plates and other assorted debris. Powerboats, airboats, jet skis, and kayakers raced down the narrow creeks and disturbed all the wildlife.

We fished together every weekend, but I started hating to go because of his drinking. Most of the fond memories I have occurred on the *water* with my boys. I felt the need to test myself on the *water*, and that is why I hunted alone until they were older. I was incensed at the indifference of crabbers who left abandoned crab traps, which became navigational hazards. No place was without evidence of man's disregard for nature.

POLLUTION

Much later, I became aware of how polluted the waters had become. My doctor said, "Stay out of Mobile Bay with your lung problems. You could not fight off vibrio vulnificus if you caught it." Vibrio vulnificus is a flesh-eating bacterium that thrives in warm saltwater. Its infections remind me of the bubonic plague, with skin blisters that are often purple. In 2012 several people died from infections through open wounds, and one from eating raw oysters. I admit that I am scared to death of vibrio. It is a hell of a way to die. The book *Silent Spring* alerted us to the growing contamination of our *air* and *water*.

Now I think back on those days when Dad and I seined our own bait with a two-man seine and when James, my brother-in-law, and I and my two boys shrimped with our sixteen-foot net. It seemed to me that nature's bounty was diverse and abundant.

Once, on Fish River, Dad, Redd, and I went shrimping in the mouth of Weeks Bay, and Dad fell overboard drunk. He fell right in the middle of the net with the motor still running. He surfaced and screamed at me to turn it off, but I didn't know how. Finally, I got it stopped. Redd stood up on the bow of the boat and kept yelling, "Charge, charge."

When I think of the water, my thoughts go back to the days of building blinds with my boys, of hunting wood ducks in Little Catfish Bayou, and of my last hunt with my son Tom, when I finally shot a redhead duck. I think back on the few good times with the Emperor in Smith's Bayou, with Mom in Mama's ditch, in Blakely River with my brother-in-laws, and especially of me alone in Lake Texoma, Texas, when my life almost ended.

I am drawn to the *water*, and it has helped to define who I am. I am a man of the bayous and the bays, a lover of all that ride the waves. It is my sanctuary, my retreat from a world I no longer respect. Age and infirmity make my outings less frequent, but my mind, as agile as ever, clings even more to the memories that I hold precious.

Man is failing his obligation to *water*. And that shame I share. No waterway is as it was; all are spoiled. If I go into the bayous again, I only pray that I can find some area that reminds me of my youth, of a time when the world seemed stable and promising, of a time when I was proud to be a man full of vigor and purpose, of a time when the banks were lined with trees instead of houses and debris, when the *water* was pure, blue, and inviting.

Fire

I dream that I am bound at the stake
As a black-robed figure appears with *fire*.
He grins as he bends down and sets the blaze.
Sadly, I recognize him as my father.

BANK FAILURES

Frank Milton sat by the phone and waited, praying for a call that he did not expect to receive. Nothing was as it had been since a beast called the Great Depression had come with a vengeance and transformed every economic entity. The railroad was the backbone of his farm and timber community, and he had been brakeman for the L & N Railroad for most of his life.

What had happened? He didn't know; he was a brakeman, not an economist. Some said it was the stock market crash of 1929. He had heard stories of wealthy men who jumped out of plush offices to their deaths. Frank had no money in the market, but he did have a few acres of land that had been taken by the bank. A good friend had turned Frank down for a loan, saying that his hands were tied from higher up. Then that bank failed, as did hundreds of others.

The phone call would not come. That he knew. Others were also engaged in a telephone vigil: engineers, conductors, and other brakemen with more seniority. He was young but the odd man out. He hadn't had time to save, and without the land, there was nothing left. He had hoped to court Mary Wynn, but she would have problems of her own, and what future could she expect from a young, uneducated, penniless, unemployed brakeman.

He knew his train would be coming through town. It came once a week now, when before it had come every day. He would go down to the tracks for one last nostalgic look. The conductor could not stop in time, and Frank Milton, who loved Mary Wynn, lay mangled in the bed of the tracks.

THE DECLINE PROGRESSES

My father died during the time of the twin wars of Iraq and Afghanistan. In World War II, he had tried to enlist and become a flyer, but he was refused because of his eyesight. He tried another service but with the same result. At ninety-four, he had an eye operation that left him with little more than light perception. I think from his explosive nature and his boxing days in the town alleyways he always wanted to be a warrior.

His parsimony was legendary; it was much beyond thrift. Anyone who knew him remarked how tight he was with money, and I would add also with compassion and love. One of his nurses remarked, "If you stuck coal up his ass, he would shit diamonds." Wherever he went, he would utilize the available resources. If someone bought him lunch, he would keep the Styrofoam container, wash it out, and reuse it. There was a stack of containers on both sides of his freezer that rose to the ceiling.

Even more unusual was his lunch—the same lunch for most of his life. He would open a can of Campbell's vegetable beef soup and pour it into a bowl, which he would then put in the refrigerator. After an hour, he would get it out and scrape the fat off the surface. This ritual was designed to keep his blood free-flowing. I don't remember exactly when I began to realize that my father was losing touch with reality. His moods caused him to break into a rage over discontent between the races. His treatment of Mother worsened after such an episode.

Gradually, I noticed that some exchanges with his clients turned bad, especially when his bill surprised a client. I remember on more than one occasion him screaming at the client that he was getting value for his money. Many of the regulars endured the abuse and stayed, but some, like the forester, left. And a departure would always trigger an explosion. Mom would try to smooth it over but it never worked.

"What's wrong, honey?" she'd ask.

"Harris, that no-good SOB, quit me."

"Well, maybe it's for the best. He was always complaining. We'll get by."

"What the hell do you know?"

"I work all day, cook, and do housework."

"Shut your damn mouth. If I want your damn opinion, I'll ask for it."

Mom would start crying. He would start drinking and go into the living room to fume, and then he would come back at her. I hated the Emperor for his treatment of her. Everything he did was oriented to the accumulation of wealth. Insofar as Mother and I could help, we were useful. Mother did all the real work, and I typed the returns as he sat in meditation for much of the day.

It was a long-standing irritation that made him that way. I call it Depression fatigue. His memory of those sad times—of a sweet potato or a ladle of onion soup for dinner—never left him, and he constantly prepared for the next calamity. *Fire* can be seen in many guises. A temper that simmers then boils, an argument mildly advanced that turns vengeful, a smile that becomes a scowl, a face tightened—these were the signs I remember.

He was mercurial in his moods, trenchant in his defense of himself, and always ready to bestow blame but never allowing any criticism. I trembled with every encounter over grades or chores. I felt like Oliver Twist, who asked for just a little more. I just wanted a tidbit of something like an occasional expression of love. As he was lying in his hospital bed, restrained against his will, he said, "I love you, son." Finally, after all those years, it was nice to hear. How could you love such a man? I don't know, but I did.

I am a southerner first and independent. In fact, I laughingly tell my children that I am an anachronistic, iconoclastic, rugged southern existentialist individual in this sense of the definition, like the Emperor. I am southern to the point of regretting that I could not have ridden with General Bedford Forrest as did my great-great-grandfather in the Sixth Georgia Cavalry. Also, my South is my refuge as an ideal, not from acre to acre but from border to border. Twelve southerners wrote of the distressing effects of progress in the book *I'll Take My Stand*. History proved them right. Industrialization ruined the agrarian South and destroyed its belief system, its culture, and largely its promise.

As I said, the civil rights struggle was one way to mark the phases of my life as they passed: first with the "She ded" comment, then my father's anger at the Bloody Bridge, the Parks incident, the Black Power symbol, the Wallace stand-aside order at the school, and the constant appearance and inflammatory rhetoric of the black religious leaders who carved out their own infamous legacy. All of this was *fire*. It will continue to escalate as the mutual distrust between black and white will never be resolved, as was clearly evident in Ferguson, Missouri.

I say to all the players, I foresee the outcome, but I am tired and do not wish to be held hostage by your antics any longer. I do not wish any more phases of my life to be colored by the bellicose nature of both sides. According to the tarot card, man is driven by two horses—one white, one black—each pulling against the other so that progress is impossible unless the charioteer can take control and make them work as one. Where is man's charioteer?

My life has been difficult, with many mistakes, many lost opportunities. I have been at war with my father and myself. In life there are always lingering questions, a feeling of incompleteness, unanticipated problems in business or love, a quarrel with a neighbor—nagging, interrupting, irritating impediments to a complete self. I am no stranger to such discontent and neither was my dad.

I am unpredictable and withdrawn, and I much prefer my own company. I am harder to know than even I dreamed possible. I still search for the real me. Death resolves most minor matters but leaves no opportunity for redress.

I am not afraid of life but am confused by it and the religious implications. It is an intense matter, as one can clearly see now in the struggles between the various factions in the cradle of civilization. This is a world without harmony, a world affected by an unseen but ever-present invader that I call progress. By its fast pace and demands on time, it lessens the opportunity for any serious contemplation of someone called God. Yet belief in him is the residual need. I suspect that the ability to question the plan was another gift; otherwise, why would man alone in the animal kingdom have reason and, by extension, free will.

I am a Leo, and we are always masculine. It is the lion symbol and all that goes with it, but even a lion will carefully choose his ground. Mine is a war on two fronts with my father and myself. I have almost died twice by drowning, once was caught in a quicksand-like nutria bog, and once had a gun put to my chest and the trigger pulled. I do not fear death, but I do get pissed at the thought of it, and I fear the manner of my death.

Death by *fire* scares me the most—to burn alive. And I don't for a moment believe that it purifies or redeems, as did the Inquisition. It is a horrid method of disposal. I wonder about the difference between mortal death and religious death, but it is a fleeting consideration. No doubt it is the latter that should most be feared, and that fear is a cornerstone for religious opinion.

I miss my mother. In my childhood, she was the buffer between him and me. His alcoholic tantrums scared me as a kid, but she would hold me, soothe me, and say, "This will pass quickly, son." Usually the tirade was short but intense. It caused me to run away from home a couple of times.

Almost anything would trigger the outbreaks, especially visits by my aunt. She constantly berated him about Mother. I remember one time that they argued about a movie.

"Take her to the movie," she said. "She slaves for you."

"Mind your own damn business."

"She wants you to take her, damn it."

"Can't afford it. Let her watch TV."

"Crap, you got more gold than Midas."

"Go home, you ain't wanted here."

GOING HOME

Mom deserved better than she got. She would work for him all day in the hot garage office, then cook his supper, wash the dishes by hand, iron his clothes, and get me ready for school. Mother was also a good gardener. We grew potatoes and even sunflowers. She never complained. He sat on his ass and watched TV. He constantly masturbated his pipe by jerking it off with Dill pipe cleaners.

One night, the Emperor came into my little bedroom and made me come into the kitchen. Mom was crying. He told me that they were breaking up, and I had to choose between them. I chose my mother. He went berserk and passed out. The next day, it was as if nothing had happened.

I remember a time that almost broke my mother's heart. I had been home for a weekend from Auburn University and was headed back with two friends in the car. We were in a hurry to return, and as I crested a hill, I realized that I could not stop. The car plowed into the rear of one of the cars in a funeral procession. It was chaos for a while. No one was seriously injured, but both cars were severely damaged.

After the officer had written a report, I went to a nearby home and called Dad. He told me to stay there, and he was hollering and screaming obscenities at me. I figured that I would let him calm down, so my friends and I hitched a ride back to Auburn.

Over the next couple of months, I tried to explain why I had to leave. We were in finals at school. I didn't mention that I had a date. The Emperor would not listen to any excuses. I had left him with a mess to clean up. He immediately stopped sending me money. As a result, I had to find a new place to live.

A friend of mine introduced me to a friend of his at a party. The man asked if I liked Johnny Cash. I replied that I loved to listen to Cash. I said, "He's my favorite, my man in black." He said that he had a two-room apartment where I could stay with him if I would audit some classes for him should he have to leave. He mentioned something about family trouble in the country.

So I stayed with him, and nightly we would listen to Johnny Cash. Thanks to another friend, I got a job as a waiter. Still, it wasn't enough to pay tuition or other expenses; it was just enough for beer money.

My friend and I drank a lot of moonshine. I had to audit several of his classes for a week while he was away. His family had some farming interests, and his father had been killed. When he came back, we drank hard shine. This, he told me, was the best made. He lit a cap full of shine, and it burned with a blue flame.

I was fired as a waiter because I refused to bow down to a drunken customer. It became obvious that I could not stay at college, so I said good-bye to my good friend and hitched a ride home.

HOME, SWEET HOME

Dad was in his downtown office when I got there. I said, "Hi, Dad. I'm home." He turned around in his swivel chair. Then he took his pipe and carefully laid it in the ashtray. For a moment he did nothing but stare at me. Then he spoke. "Go see your mother. I'll be there soon. Get what is yours, and get."

I said, "Dad, I know I should have stayed." I tried to explain about finals, and I added, "Can't we be friends now that I'm home?"

His answer stunned me, and the thought of it even after all these years sends shivers down my spine. If I had been shot, I don't think the impact would have hurt as much. "You have no home."

Mom was overjoyed to see me until she realized I was packing a small suitcase. "What are you doing?"

"The Emperor has banished me. I love you, Mother. I'll be fine." I hugged her and went outside. She pleaded with me not to go. She said she could calm him down, but I knew it wouldn't work. I told her, "If I stay, he'll only hurt us both. It will be better if I leave."

After I had walked away, I looked back. Mom was on her knees in the front yard. She was crying. When I think back on that episode, I realize that I had committed the ultimate sin, according to Dad. Even though he settled the damages for a small sum, and we were fortunate that no one was injured, in his mind my transgression was unforgivable: I had cost him money.

When I was older and had my children, I told them that they would always have a home. No matter what tribulation came their way, I wanted them to know that there was a sanctuary for them to come to. I hoped that would be a comfort for them, for I can speak with the assurance that I know what it is like to be abandoned.

The only happiness that I had with him was fishing, especially at the point on a piece of property that he owned—a point on a little creek with an oxbow bay. Mom begged him to keep it for her kids, but he sold it soon after she died. Fishing and listening to *Amos and Andy* on the old Philco radio were the only pleasant memories I have of the three of us in that old trailer.

CONFLICTS REVISITED

TV began to highlight the civil rights movement. At first, white populations hardly noticed the growing animosity and determination for change by the Negro. The days of Uncle Remus,

Little Black Sambo, and the old colored woman named Rosie, who tipped her hat to a young boy, had changed. It was hard to envision the civil strife that would follow the rise to prominence of the supposed oppressed and the change toward a minority status for the white populace. Other races clamored for recognition as immigration control failed miserably from neglect, greed, and a benign but stupid belief that America can absorb the world. This is most noticeable in the unresolved and continuous border conflicts with Mexico and Central America.

An Argument

My father's office consisted of two tables cluttered with law books filled with case histories and codes, and his chair was piled high with newspapers and magazines relating to investments or estate planning, all of which were donated by his friends or broker. In the working area of his desk was the ever-present ledger in which he wrote each day's increase in values. An old, broken, blue-wing teal decoy was next to the typewriter. Occasionally we would enjoy a temporary truce that quickly dissipated.

He turned to face me as I entered the room and sat down in an old armchair. "What do you want?" he asked.

"No more of your get-rich-quick schemes for us."

"You ungrateful little shit. Someday you will be sorry."

"Stop, leave my wife and me in peace."

"Get the hell out and don't come back."

"I said my piece."

I left, but I still remember his comment: "Someday you will be sorry."

I still have the residual feeling that I did not know him, that my own father was more of an acquaintance than a dad and more of a pretender to be my benefactor than he really was, but later I found out that I was wrong. I recall Kahlil Gibran's comment "You can never leave your pain without regret."

The Twelfth House

I was never much into astrology, the sun in the twelfth house, Apollo worship, or a desire to bathe in the sun, to run naked and thus display an egocentric contempt for the world. Yet, if I had been interested in astrology, I would have been comfortable in the twelfth house: the home of the subconscious. Those of us who are introspective and abide loneliness choose the last house. It is a place absolutely suited to an existentialist. Without a doubt, this would have been my father's house as well. I have known people whose lives are orchestrated by the alignment of stars and planets. There is even a stock market theory that coincides with astrological projections. As I said before, if I believed.

Dad and the Depression

He was a complicated man—a man of conviction, determined to stay on track toward his goals. None dare impede his progress. He never offered a warm, tender look back, but was instead an uncaring, propelled, egocentric individual whose intensity lit up every situation. He often spoke of his days at college when he worked in the school library and was on the boxing team. Tuition was always a headwind for him, and he was always in arrears, yet he toughed it out.

It was during this time that he became somewhat of a ladies' man, which led the Emperor to marry several times. He met his first wife at a dance party, and after they married, they danced at the famous Aragon Ballroom in Chicago, Illinois, where in Aeolian Hall in Midtown Manhattan, Paul Whiteman played my favorite Gershwin tune, "Rhapsody in Blue." It was arranged by Ferde Grofe, who wrote "The Grand Canyon Suite," which was used in cigarette commercials.

Dad lost his wife and drifted and drank for a while before returning to Mobile. He said his loved one and young child would have been alive had she not contracted peritonitis, for penicillin had not been available.

In all of the marriages there was a common theme: his wives all loved to dance, including my dear mother. Dad said he loved the music and particularly the big bands, like Dorsey, Kaiser, Kemp, and Miller. Further, he said that he loved the oneness of being when two persons blending into each other.

His first real job in Mobile was working at the shipyard as an auditor. Eventually, he felt he knew enough to go into business for himself. During that time, he met and married my mother. I came along a year later, and when I was five, we moved to the Eastern Shore, where Dad set up his accounting practice.

Near the end he had imaginary dances in his living room with my mother. He even called my son Tom in the wee hours to say, "Hey, Topperererrrr, listen to this." It was usually some Glenn Miller ballroom dance that Tom could hear faintly in the background.

The Emperor, reexamined

The Emperor had love in his heart but hate in his actions. He disguised the love so well. Such a dichotomy! Everything he did was for the love of us, and every action he took was draconian. I never understood his motives; I never saw past the smokescreens. But I learned to tough it out and to "be beholden to no man." I hope in the end that pleased him. He died a lonely, broken man, and I compare his life to King Lear's, in a way. Unfortunately, I deserve a measure of Lear's comments about children, such as, "How sharper than a serpent's tooth is it to have a thankless child."

Yet, for all that I did or didn't do in life, I shall triumphantly ride the tailwind of my last breath straightaway into heaven or hell. I tried to understand him, but it wasn't until near his death that I could begin to appreciate how disorder destroys a personality. All that I had heard and studied about the Great

Depression seemed to begin to fall in place. It was déjà vu to him but something new to me.

It was 2008–2009, banks began to fail here and abroad, unemployment soared, and airline and auto and homebuilding industries teetered on the brink of bankruptcy. On some blocks, one out of every four houses was in foreclosure, and even states began to issue IOUs to pay debts. I remember a conversation I had with the Emperor near the end.

"Dad, things are getting bad. Banks are toast."

"This is child's play. In the old days, Dillinger was a hero. Even Bonnie and Clyde seemed like folks."

"Dad, tell me about the Dust Bowl."

Dad went on about the great dust clouds of topsoil that depressed all the people and destroyed farms. "Failure to rotate crops was the cause," he said. "Dumb bastards got what they deserved. Did you ever get in a bread line?"

Then he lit into me. He said that real men would hunt or fish first and emphasized that real men don't take a dole. "People lost their land, even your grandmother. And they lost something else."

"What?"

"Their minds. The Depression was hard."

He went on and on about the shantytowns, the lack of jobs, the lack of laughter, and how some made tea out of grasses and weeds like dandelion.

"What one word stands out in your mind?" I asked.

"*Lean*, those were lean times."

He went on saying that there were no fat people. Their faces were drawn taut like a damp trampoline, and there was no twinkle in their eyes, just a catatonic stare. Dad called it a squabble economy.

"Squabble economy, what's that?" I asked.

"Argue over everything, even a penny."

"I guess it was tough."

Then these last few comments of his really hurt me: "It made me hard, and God bless the fucking Depression, for that but for nothing else. It brought a *fire* in the will out of me. When I saw those railroad men throw dirt on my dead daddy, dressed in the only overalls that he had, I knew it was survival time. It has been that ever since. I have no regrets for being tough, but I do have one disappointment."

"What's that?"

"That you ain't as tough as I am."

"Don't bet on it; you will lose."

He loved to play lawyer and had sued some of his neighbors over trespassing, dogs barking, bright lights, noise, and almost anything that could be covered under the statutes of law. He pleaded and won many of the cases himself.

THE DECLINE ACCELERATES

Dad loved the sun, and it gave him a bronzed look—almost a patina—out of which his gray stubble and fierce blue eyes would emerge. He reminded me of the mad mystic Rasputin in the time of Czar Nicholas II. Rasputin had such a domineering look.

Near the end, Dad tormented my kids. He called them daily and many times demanded that they come and take care of him. He cursed them, but he never called me. I was impervious to plea, to bargain, to entrapment, to promise. I had seen the snake strike many times and knew its moves. As he and I had been for so much of our lives, at his end, we were still engaged in a battle to the death.

I had seen his temper run acerbic and bellicose; he became a screaming, demanding, demented lunatic. Once he was trying to teach me how to fly fish. I wasn't careful and caught him in the back of his shirt. He called me a "stupid, little shit" and said that I could have put his eyes out.

"I'm sorry, Dad," I said.

"Yes, you are. Thank your stars that it wasn't my eye."

We went on for a while. I got the hang of the fly presentation, and we caught some nice bluegills and shellcrackers. When we got back to Cliff's Landing, a man came over to help Dad with his motor. Dad was drunk and asked the fellow about the black patch over his eye. The man replied that he had been fly fishing with a friend a couple of years earlier and that his friend's fly caught him in the eye, which he later lost. On the way home, I caught hell. Dad tongue-lashed me for an hour.

Déjà Vu

We are accelerating into another depression. It is June of 2009, and many banks have failed and numerous businesses are bankrupt. There is a feeling of gloom on some streets in America, and many homes are in foreclosure. Even a couple of states are near bankruptcy. The contagion has spread around the globe; the world, it seems, is in free fall and decay. It must have seemed the same to Dad in the Great Depression.

He was forced to weave his way out of the Depression by sheer guts and ability, and he died as the near-depression began. If he were here, I know I would get a lecture. He would say, "Ain't nobody gonna help you. You got to tough it out alone and be hard on yourself and others so that they respect you." He would go on to say, "A pussy don't survive a depression, boy. Don't be one."

I have always believed in the cyclicality of events, and I understand the economic cycles that are supposed to control our lives. Dad was born headed into a depression and died still headed into another. He was the *depressions' child*. He toughed it out. Power to him, I say. I can't condone his meanness, but he was an achiever, and he broke down many a softie along the way.

Family Land

Sometimes I think of clans when I think back on the railroad community where Dad grew up. There were some nefarious types, as you might expect in hard times. The timberlands around the railroad tracks were in demand because of the timber and the rumor of oil. Land was sold for as little as sixteen dollars an acre because of the times and the decline of rail freight traffic. Today that damn land would sell for thousands of dollars an acre.

My father was not a visionary at that time and had not honed his business skills. He was involved in selling the family lands, because his mother was desperate for cash. There were nasty fights between him and some relatives that were involved in the transaction. A family fortune was lost for sixteen dollars an acre in the Depression. It was land that I passed over on the Hummingbird train.

I read the letters between the lawyers, the family, and the forester, and in my opinion there may have been some timberland income that was unaccounted for in the beginning. Of course, if that income had flowed through as it should have, it might have prevented the sale. Now it seems ludicrous that the land should have been sold for what is a pittance today. Yet that was the Depression; the mind-set and the purchasing power of the dollar were different. Unfortunately, it made sense to the folks at the time.

The cemetery where so many of mine relatives lie was land that my father and grandfathers hunted on. The railroad sinew that parts ancestral land on either side is a painful reminder of my roots. Strange the heat that bitterness between family members can engender. Being called a name or faulted for acting on another's behalf causes searing pain. The thing called money fuels the *fire*.

ECONOMIC EQUALITY

Now is a different time, but a troubled one. America is under attack by the hordes of invaders that cross our borders. The copper lady invites more, not from the age-old discard of the Monroe Doctrine but from a philosophy centered on the lofty ideal first mentioned in the Constitution: all men are created equal. On religious grounds, I do not argue the point. Yet, if we consider *equal* in isolation, then fine. However, this is the crux: all men are not created equal from an economic standpoint. The philosophical question is, should they be? If one man works but another refuses—that is, one is a "have" by choice and one a "have-not" by choice—does that suggest a need to redistribute wealth? I say no. *Hell no.* (The infirm, blind, disabled, mentally challenged, and elderly are excepted.)

Some argue that being born into poverty changes the equation. I do not deny that may make the outcome tougher to achieve, but all can find an avenue to success. The philosophy triumphs: if you work hard and succeed, kudos to you; if you just get by, then expect to just get by. I fault no man for the accident of birth, for his color, his creed, or his infirmities, but I do fault him for his attitude and belligerence, and the ensuing conflict that he causes.

I speak truth! I have been poor, without friends, alone on the brink of giving up, yet I pulled myself up out of the abyss and gathered the fortitude out of my gut, because I had to make my life count; otherwise there was no point to the attempt. Later I was lucky to find an exceptional partner in life, and I lay the great majority of my achievements at her feet.

The Emperor, Continued

I called Dad the Emperor because his directives had to be followed, but with age I was able to break free of him. I knew the game, for once he had offered me a silver Rolls-Royce if I would work with him and postpone getting married. Later, as he was dying, he played the pity card, saying, "I need you to take care of me. I'll pay." This I had heard before. He told me to tough it out and stand alone. He never gave my children or me presents, and he made my childhood hell.

I replied, "You might as well offer seashells. I know you can't part with money. Hire a damn nurse."

"I'll pay you. I need you now."

"Yes, now but not before. Lousy record."

"You are a cruel, hard-hearted bastard."

"Dad, you made me that way."

There would always be friction between us in both thought and deed. Always a *fire* to be quelled and naturally a deep, gut-wrenching remorse that inevitably followed. In things except being a father, he was brilliant.

The sun is bright today, and I welcome the warmth. Much of my life has been in shadow, in cold, sometimes heavy with a deep sorrow. It was brought on by my inability to understand or appreciate a father who gave no quarter, permitted no insurrection, was the absolute emperor. Yet that is past. I can wrap the warm memories around me, and though they are few, the embers suffice to dispel the chill. Yes, it is bright today because I know that I was successful in the things that mattered: family, purpose, knowledge, and a sense of self-sufficiency.

I have to allow my financial success to grow, to nurture it as I would a garden, for this success must be passed on and inculcated by instruction and deeds to those I love. What I did with Dad or without him I did because of him, and that debt is one each child owes his father.

DEATH

Both of my parents' deaths were difficult to view, yet death is only the logical expression of the most basic laws of the universe, such as the second law of thermodynamics, which says simply that things move from order to disorder. All things decay, or as the Buddhist would offer, all is impermanent and interdependent. Yet this can be a call to arms, to boldly leave the shadow and enjoy the remaining sunshine, to be, as my dear uncle Redd said once, warm.

Death suggests again our elements, and I recall, perhaps from the Tibetan philosophy, something about the dissolution of the body being a retreat to the elements as soul to breath, to *air*, as decomposition to *fire* (consumption), *water* (liquefaction), and *earth*, as the ultimate repository. And at death the soul will be in transition to another incarnation or on a course for Nirvana or maybe just red-shifting into space. Many theories discuss near-death experiences. As I was drowning, I recall nothing but a fierce will to survive. Then there was no look-back option for me.

Something like that I think I remember. Yet out of the disorder will come order, the originality of the thing, ash, dirt, *earth*—that old mumbo jumbo about dust to dust. "So long, Dad" was not much to say to a man who had lived and slaved for ninety-four years. He would know my intent, because in our previous conversations, at least for the last few years, the words were cold, harsh, and spiteful. Yet this simple comment was made soft but audible, an economical expression that said what needed to be said. He would have found the words comforting and warm. I hope that forgiveness, like a cloak, can bring warmth if and when it comes to me.

RACE OF IRON

I admit my pessimism. My admiration for my country as a beacon for the world has diminished. Every day I wonder how this great achievement in ethics and purpose could have been so violated over time.

In his *Work and Days*, Hesiod said that there were five races of humans, beginning with the golden race and ending with the last and worst race, which he called the Race of Iron. In that ancient time, Hesiod offered that the last race would be one of shame and retribution. So by default we are that last and worst race—last and unfortunately not best. Indeed, that is our shame.

THE NATURE OF MAN

Wars are a reflection of *fire* in the psyche of men. Yet Sartre said that "hell is other people." I often wonder if hell existed before heaven was created. Considering the basic nature of man, it would seem the greater necessity. My father saw many wars but never got to fight in one. So he made his own war between him and me. Man will never eschew war, as it is in his subconscious as an archetype, perhaps from the days of Cain and Abel. There is always a need to triumph in your viewpoint, no matter the means, and I wonder if the final battle will be at Megiddo or at some intergalactic stopover. We are a species destined to disorder, and it is this ravenous, mechanistic monster named progress that propels us toward our end.

Air

Imagine the soul borne on the *air*,
The mind's essence finally free to travel,
Light as a blown dandelion buffeted by;
A cosmic breath I cannot understand.

A SONG OF LOVE

As a young child on Kentucky Street, I went to a kind of Bible school with my grandmother. It was in the church in which I was later married to my wife, Ginny. We didn't know each other then, though we lived only a few blocks apart. As children we went to the same playground, the same church, and the same movie theater, and we walked the same streets with friends. The Roosevelt Theater was my favorite place. It always had a serial after the movie, and my favorite was *Flash Gordon*.

Even now I remember the song we used to sing in the Bible school, "Hi-Lili, Hi-Lo." It is about love bringing both joy and sadness. After the last heated comments with Dad, that tune kept playing in my mind, and it surfaces even now. I can say that I have been equally intense in my experiences with both love and sadness, and sometimes they even seem simultaneous.

I AM SAVED

The day that the jetliner crash-landed on the Hudson River, when the rescued talked of the cold wind and frigid *water* and their near encounter with hypothermia, I thought of my own total immersion in the near-freezing waters of Lake Texoma, Texas. The sight of the *water* far above me made me see it momentarily as a roof—no sky, just a roof of rippling *water* with sharp, swordlike rays of light streaming down into the abyss.

First, I am lucky that the hunter saw me go over, as he was way down the lake in a small skiff. When I finally surfaced, I saw him pulling out of his blind. I managed to stay calm, despite the hip waders that weighed me down. I had the presence of mind to cut the straps loose from my belt. In the time that it took for him to get to me, my mind wandered, and I thought I might swim to shore. I would have died.

I have forgotten my camouflaged savior's name; all I remember is that he was from Oklahoma. I think of that day often, of his daring and my calm determination to live constantly on my mind. I have been a hunter, a fisherman, and a resident of the Gulf Coast—always a man with a love for the *water*.

I think back on my trip on the Hummingbird alone. It was my first real excursion, my first train ride. It was an exhilarating experience and the first with responsibility for myself. I think of my many varied experiences and my thirst for knowledge both empirical and academic. It may be said of me that in life I had a colorful ride. The little railroad crossing at Owassa, Alabama, where many of my relatives are buried, brings a rush of emotion, with the realization that the railroad is a part of who I became. I have told my children to check on the graves of their ancestors occasionally to be sure that their rest remains undisturbed.

THE TIMES—A PERSPECTIVE

A song about love and sadness and the highs and lows of love reverberates in my memory. I think of the White House occupation by the black president, the old black lady who used to show respect to a young boy who could care less, and the black man who succinctly pointed out by implication that my South was dead. No question, the civil rights struggle colored us all as did the Depression long before the ongoing drama.

On October 29, 1929, the bottom fell out of the stock market. As a former stockbroker, I can understand the mad rush for the exits, the feeling that the wealth effect was forever gone. Some say it was margin calls that drove so many to dive out of windows, but surely it was the sudden loss of pride. You may consider it vengeance from one of the deadly sins.

Horrid as it was, it was just the prelude to the hell to come from such events as the Dust Bowl and the groundswell of civil rights that the Roosevelt Administration fostered. Hobo towns were spawned near the rails. The Great Depression brought the nursemaid government directly into their lives. Even now it seems that government for some is a substitute for both mother and father.

MUSINGS

I miss the days with my cousin Denny when we swam in the Santa Rosa Sound of Pensacola, Florida, and picked up sand dollars and conch shells from the beach. I also miss the happy days with my uncle Redd, when we discussed the mysteries of Masonry over Pabst Blue Ribbon beer. Now, as I strain for enough *air* to buoy tired and diseased lungs, I think how lucky I was to marry a southern lady, a woman as fine as I could have hoped to find, and how proud I am of my three children and six grandchildren.

I wonder why I can't sense the presence of the Observer anymore. I don't feel him watching me as I did in each of the cardinal points of my life. Also, I think of that damn Depression, the great calamity that made my father intolerant and brutal and made some distant railroad relatives consider suicide. It humbled all of them and washed over me every day, like an encroaching tide, until it nearly claimed me as well, even though I was years removed from the original tribulation.

When I was in high school, Dad ordered me to find a job. He kept pressuring me, but I really didn't try until I mentioned that to a friend, who had invited me to go rabbit hunting with him. "Mike, I need a job," I said.

"Father on your case?"

"Yeah, how did you know?"

"Figures, everybody knows how ruthless he is. Kids will talk, you know."

RELIGIOUS HODGEPODGE

My friend said that he would talk to his boss, who ran a faith-healing institute. One day later in the week, he said, "Boss wants to meet you." We went to see his employer, who introduced himself as Reverend Timothy.

"I understand that you are near top in your class," Rev. Timothy said. "In literature, history, and other subjects. True?"

"Yes sir, but not in math."

"I'll worry about the math. You think that you can read manuscripts that I write. Maybe give me ideas from literature or history that fit."

"Yes sir."

Reverend Timothy hired me. I found out that he wrote religious courses on marriage and related subjects. After he wrote them, other high school classmates would mimeograph, collate, and mail them to a list of addresses from all over the world. Sometimes a client would come to him for special instruction.

For about a year, I worked there. Most times I would read a course and make suggestions about how the subject had been handled by great writers, and I would find text and quotes for him. I also had to kill his pet Angora rabbits whenever he wanted one for dinner. I would shoot them in the head with a .22-caliber, single-shot rifle and dress them for his dinner. Sometimes I had to kill more than one to accommodate his guests. I hated that part of my job. Later I bought the rifle from him when he was strapped for cash.

Most of what I read I thought was juvenile. I could have done better, but people paid good money to read the crap, and he would get glowing letters from those who said it changed their lives. Maybe he meant well. I thought him a charlatan, but as a teenager, I had no experience for making a judgment. One thing was certain: he was not well versed in literature. That is where I made a difference. Even in high school I was deep into books. After all, I spent my summers in the library, trying to get away from Dad as much as possible.

Years later I found out that the Emperor had a meeting with Reverend Timothy. I asked him why.

"I heard some things about his operation," he said. "You needed to work; otherwise I would have made you quit."

"What was the problem?" I asked.

"Those damn rabbits and your low salary."

"What happened?"

"We reached an agreement."

I know now that is why someone else took over shooting the rabbits. Dad had heard about tularemia in rabbits. That was all he needed to know, even though it was largely confined to the West and to wild animals in particular. He also thought I had been affected by Timothy's ramblings. Yet there was nothing to grasp. His courses were a network of mixed musings from various religions and meant nothing.

The only thing that I came away with was a realization that I didn't know if there is a heaven; but I did know there is a hell. I did not know enough then or now to be overly critical. Yet, despite the claims that God is omnipresent, omnipotent, and omniscient, some of what Timothy suggested God could do seemed preposterous and simply unnecessary. All of the courses were designed for lost souls who needed a designed belief system.

Yet he was my employer. I did what I was told, and on more than one occasion a course may have had lines inspired by a bored high school kid who was just beginning his own search for purpose.

MUSIC

I remember the big bands, early country and western, and classical music. My first introduction to classical was Rachmaninoff's Piano Concerto No. 2. I played it again and again. Dad and Mom would listen to Guy Lombardo, Kay Kaiser, Eddy Duchin, Hal Kemp, and others, and on the weekends they would dance together into the wee hours in our living room. Later in life, I adopted Gershwin's "Rhapsody in Blue" as my personal favorite, as the theme song for my life has been truly a rhapsody in blue.

After Mom died, he would listen to the oldies on his 78-rpm player and whirl around the living room with his arms outstretched as if he were holding her. Every night he would continue this ritual of dancing with a ghost. He loved her and idolized her but seldom showed her tenderness. I don't believe that he understood that love requires respect.

FAREWELL, MY LOVE

Mother's cancer was large, inoperable, and slow growing, and by the time it was discovered, nothing could be done. She was in pain—constant, unbearable, unrelenting pain. I was a regional manager in Texas, but I flew home almost every weekend for two years because Dad would call and say, "It will be this weekend. You better come. She will want you here."

Always, it was the same. He bitched and moaned that he had to care for her, change her, clean up accidents, and lose his usual but important routine. It got so bad that he actually paid a nurse to come part time as Mom was demanding more morphine. One weekend, she did die. I was there as her last breath exploded, and perhaps with it her soul blew past me. I wonder if the airborne soul redshifts along with the rest of us to another garden. Sweet Mother! I would no longer hear, "We will get through this with him, son."

I watched as her body was loaded into the hearse. I heard one of the attendants say, "Let's get this stiff back and go get a beer." I cursed him for his lack of respect. Death was not foreign to me. In an earlier job, I had worked in a morgue. I understood the rites of passage. Once, on a cold, snowy winter evening, I carried a stillborn through the snow and put it into the satellite morgue, which was outside of the hospital. I had admitted many dead into the morgue by myself. I would sign for the body, and with the attendant's help, place it on the steel tray. Then I would securely lock the morgue and walk back through the deep snow banks to the hospital lab.

I had seen other deaths and had watched an autopsy, so I thought I was steeled for death. Yet this was my mother, and the son of a bitch had referred to her as "the stiff."

We went to make arrangements, and Dad selected a cardboard box to bury her in, like the temporary one that they use to hold a body for cremation. I went nuts, and he finally acquiesced. As I recall, it was the only time he ever deferred to me. At my insistence, Mom was buried in a simple but sturdy pine casket. We never spoke of that day again.

She was the world to me as a child, my sunshine, my refuge, my mentor. God, how I loved her! *Vaya con dios*, Mother.

Toward the End

Toward the end, he fought hard. This was a man afraid to die who had never expressed any belief in God or made recommendation of him to me, yet in his belongings I found letters where he had quoted Scripture. He was a complex man. I didn't understand then. He was a stern, autocratic southern individualist with no noticeable religious veneer.

On his last day, he was propped up on his bed with a PICC line in his arm. He was restrained and took no notice of us. The deadly antibiotic-resistant MRSA had invaded his lungs. His head was cocked back with his eyes open and fixed on the ceiling. His eyes never left that fixed position, and I wonder if in his morphine-induced stupor he thought that he saw God. I hope so.

Later his legs became mottled and shortly thereafter he died, a little more than skin and bones. There passed a man who came from a simple railroad town and lived to see the Great Depression, a World War, the Korean War, the Vietnam War, the Cuban Missile Crisis, the Gulf wars, the 1929 and 1987 stock market crashes, wars in Iraq and Afghanistan, and the Falkland Island and Grenada conflicts. At the end, he witnessed the beginning of the Great Recession of 2008. In short, he lived a panorama of life.

I remember a quote attributed to Socrates: "Death begins in the extremities." Dad's death did, but his fear of death began in the Great Depression. He did not die easy. It had begun with his pipe smoking, which scarred his lungs and gave him emphysema. Death would have occurred sooner, but his physical regimen of trying to walk and run held the disease process in check. Gradually, he began to have serious prostate problems and then a cancer scare, but it wasn't until he developed a noticeable barrel chest that he finally quit smoking.

Each year that passed, he got worse. Then he developed macular degeneration in his eyes but still drove to the doctor's office and to the bank to deposit his money. Of course, we were petrified at the idea of a near-blind, ninety-four-year-old driving without insurance. He cared only for himself, never giving a thought to the child he might hurt by his reckless behavior.

We checked him into a hospice, but he checked himself out— still with a Foley catheter in him—because he would not pay the co-pay, which was high. Toward the end he declined and looked like a Holocaust survivor. Later he bounced off a hallway wall and passed out. The hospice nurse and a neighbor got him to the hospital, where with adequate fluid intake he responded.

Always combative, he battled the nurses, the doctor—everyone, in fact. He refused to take his medicine and absolutely refused steroids. At the end, the once proud, egocentric southerner was a sniffling infant. I have never seen a man so deathly afraid of death itself. His arms were pencil thin, and his face had wrinkles like deep canyons across a plain. He kept repeating, "We are a happy family," as if desperately trying to convince himself that we were. But the tears gave him away. His hoary gray hair was thin in front yet full in back. We had to give him *water* through a syringe.

I thought he was gone, and then he grabbed my arms and those of my son Tom and started yelling, "I can still make money for this family." He kept repeating the phrase, and the color returned to his face. His purpose in life had been announced. I knew at that time he longed for his desk, his ledgers, and the rolling hills and sand traps of the nearby golf course.

The next day my daughter, Joan, came and sat with him. As she fed him, she held his hand and told him that she loved him. That was her last positive memory of Dad. He was beaming—happy to see her. I think he loved Joan a great deal, maybe seeing my mother in her, but he was not a man comfortable with expressing love. It had always been left unsaid, but his face at the sight of all the kids was radiant. He loved them and, in his fashion, me as well.

When I think of Dad, I think of the heavy burden that falls on the head of a family. A man can be considered a man only if he accepts that burden and labors until all in his care are emotionally and financially secure. Dad tried in his way, and I tried in mine.

SAD TIDE

There is a wave of guilt sweeping over me as I contemplate our life together. So much angst and regret. I imagine the guilt will come and go like a tide that periodically bathes a beach with foam. I forgive him and wish as much for myself.

As he drifted away, I felt even more guilt for not being there at the end. I was headed that way, but the phone call came first. He had multiple problems, including the deadly MRSA in his lungs, and his breath could have infected me. The Hi-Lili song continues to haunt me. Yes, a song of love is a song of sadness. There were times I could have used his compassion, but I had to tough it out without him. A father who won't help is different from a father who can't help.

At the very end he was in a sitting position with his head back and his eyes open, fixed on the ceiling. His head rolled from side to side as he moaned. Not once did he recognize me nor did he answer the nurse when she said, "Sir, can you wake up and talk to me?" His arms were restrained and bruised from repeated phlebotomies, and his mouth was wide open as if to maximize the intake of *air*. His lungs made a rattling sound as if to warn the visitor to stay his distance.

This was not the man I knew. Instead, this was Everyman, who searched the horizon in his mind for some glimpse of the future, whether it be heaven or hell. Thus preoccupied, he was oblivious to all else. Death was closing in on him. It came a bit after I left to go home.

For a while, I got the runaround from the nurses, who seemed to be in an excessively defensive mood. Finally, I got a conference with the director and the two attending nurses. My son Tom was with me. I inquired about his lab work, and they were polite but reserved. I said, "Ladies, I appreciate your need to practice defensive medicine, but my family will need to make arrangements, and we are in the dark about his prognosis. Please understand that the two meanest men on the planet are here. One is dying in your critical care unit, and the other is before you inquiring about his condition. I expect a realistic answer." After that, they were a bit more forthcoming.

Dad had realized his dream. His was a true rags-to-riches story. He could have been nicer. I could have been nicer, more caring, more loving, but it would have been an act. Our personalities had been forged in combat. I had been callous, cold, unyielding, and unreasonable. Strangers brought him dinner and invited him to their houses for days. Their children gave him gifts, although he never gave mine a gift. He always had a place to go for Christmas or Easter, but never with us. We did invite him a few times, but he didn't come.

There was that time when I invited him to go with Redd and me to my hunting camp in Chatom, Alabama, for a weekend. At first he said yes, but then Redd came alone and said that Dad had changed his mind. I understood. We were still at war. However, now the nagging loss and the impossibility of redress haunt me. No tears, but I am pounded by incessant waves of guilt, crashing against the rock called me.

I am forlorn, and in this state the elements consume me. The rage is a *fire* that toasts my soul. The *earth* is without a stone marker, no opportunity for closure. The *water* haunts me as I recollect good times in Fish River and Mama's Ditch, and in the lake that was called something else before it was called Negro Lake. And *air* holds the breath of all three of us and perhaps contains my parents' souls like quarks, dark energy, or some string phenomena vibrating around me, some current like kinetic energy that I cannot see.

I think I understand the Observer. If there is a terror of hell or a joy of heaven, it is simply an elementary imagination or nothing, and if it is nothing, there is no reason to care. Is the Observer a trickster, a laughable Bugs or evil Loki? Does he get thrills from toying with mankind? It is his game and his rules.

I find it difficult to pray for Dad or me, for both of us were lost. We never understood the blueprint. I still don't, I can't deny it. I just don't understand where I fit in it. I wonder who really does. And as the guilt continues to surround me, I wonder, was I ever in control of free will? Am I now?

Following his death, I found the old Philco radio that we used to listen to *Amos and Andy*. It was in horrible condition and unplayable, yet it was a prized possession for me. It currently sits on a shelf in my man cave. I look at it daily. In its day, it was top of the line.

The *Amos and Andy* Boys

I hired two black fellows to help me clean out the garage. Dad had left hundreds of old paint cans, paving cement, oil, tar, kerosene, and all manner of flammable solvents that needed to be disposed of, including a bucket full of rusted twenty-gauge shotgun shells. When I think of the hundreds of useless items we found in his garage and closets, I am reminded of my daughter's comment that Dad was like an Egyptian Pharaoh preparing for his afterlife.

We loaded Whitecap's (one of my helpers) flatbed truck, which had no sides. Paint cans were stacked two tiers high. I told him and Conwee, his helper, "Guys, when you drive to the dump those cans are gonna fly out. Someone may get hurt."

Whitecap said, "Ah, nawsir, boss, ain't gonna hap dat away. We go slow. Hit be fine. Old Whitecap know 'bout dese things I does." He went on to tell me that he had driven a big rig for a living when he was younger.

I followed them in my car, and we hadn't gone more than thirty yards toward the dump when the first paint can came flying out, much like a projectile depth charge. I swerved off the road and picked it up and had to do this with several more cans.

I drove up behind Whitecap and Conwee. Whitecap said, "Looksee har, boss. Cans be on de truck bed."

I said nothing, but got the cans out of my car and put them back on his truck. Then I went to get the necessary permit. Whitecap and Conwee reminded me of Amos and Andy, and I had to laugh about it all the way home. It had been a family program that we all looked forward to hearing—the exploits of Kingfish in a world that had no resemblance to our own. As I said before, the civil rights struggle colored us all, as did the Depression. *Amos and Andy* was a delightful prelude to a change in status for Caucasians. They were great white actors who entertained us as Negroes.

Sometimes I imagine that I am the fool on the cliff with one foot on the edge. Hesitant, I can't decide whether to step off, confident in luck or divine promise, or to remain rooted in place. Life is so tenuous, so disturbingly brief, as my friend the engineer found out in his plunge from the Amtrak bridge into the muck of Big Bayou Canot.

The elements of the ancients—*air, fire, earth,* and *water*—still remain as pivotal reflective points of my life. *Air* is for all the wonderment, the intense need to make a leap of faith; *fire* for the longing for knowledge, the burning need to achieve; *water* for the better, more fluid times; *earth* for the idea of containment, for the idea of belonging, for the need for substance and for substantive events in my life, for the realization in the end that nothing really mattered and that all I accomplished was a private matter of no consequence to others.

I never saw a religious icon in our house—no outward expression of any belief by the Emperor, yet his eyes were fixed on the ceiling at death as if searching for the angel Raphael. I recall that if asked he would join in a blessing. I don't know why, but I thought then it was hypocritical. I asked him once why he would pray if he wasn't religious. He asked me why I wanted to know. I said that I was just curious. He said, "Truth may not help, but it can't hurt. Sometimes in business you do things because others do in this the most fucked-up country in the world. Insurance, it is."

"What do you pray for in those meetings?" I asked.

"Their business."

Dad made sense. He prayed for their business because it suited his goals. He said it couldn't hurt, which makes me wonder about heaven and hell. Perhaps these are concepts only. To me, hell is life lived badly. Heaven is life lived well with occasional unintended sidesteps. Yet if there is a heaven, we imagine it to be in the air, a place where Raphael and his buddies carry on another fellow's agenda—God's hacienda.

ANOTHER BURIAL

It is hard for me to repress the time I went to pick up my father's ashes. There was nothing to it; I simply signed a receipt in the Anatomy Lab, received the box, carried it out under my arm, got in the car, and drove home. Then I deposited the box on the mantle and stared at it as old memories crush me. Such a chill I felt. I should have shouted, cussed, and belittled him as he had done to me. Yet the words would not come, and I just stared at it. I looked at the box and realized what a formidable foe he had been. Just a thin metal box, a mini-coffin, and I was his custodian. He had been a fighter, and at the end he pulled out of his gut that last vestige of existential pureness.

It was time to scatter his ashes. Lane slowly opened the bag, poured some, and passed it to Tom. It was windy, and some of the remains got on my hands and felt greasy. I had a hard time grasping the fact that these almond-colored, chalk-like ashes belonged to dear old Dad. Sadly, I thought, *This is the closest we've gotten to a hug in many years.* I thought it appropriate to say a few words. Nothing from Psalms seemed appropriate. Instead, I recited these words of Thomas Gray: "All that beauty, all that wealth ere gave." Then I paraphrased the words of Mathew Arnold: "Eternal sadness that Sophocles heard on the Aegean." And I finished with the lines from "Invictus" that Timothy McVeigh had the warden read after his execution: "I am the master of my fate. I am the captain of my soul." Those last words might well have been Dad's.

In my own crazy conception of *air,* I see it heavy-laden with invisible things like energy, particles, dark matter, and souls, just riding on the currents. For if the law of conservation of matter is true, essence is not destroyed; souls are there just hanging out somewhere in space—redshifting along with the rest of us.

Yes, in the end, I was bitter. To have spent a lifetime in diligent study of all the philosophical questions of the day and to arrive at no better answers than did the ancient philosophers, and near the end to still be like the tarot fool poised for change and still trying to figure out the grand plan that included me.

At least Dad and I shared the thought that the world has morphed into an unrecognizable thing, especially our South. Ever since the "She ded" comment, I realized that this metamorphosis of my homeland had occurred. Rosie, Little Black Sambo, Uncle Remus, and later even Amos and Andy are all gone, all only reminders of a quieter time. They have been replaced by militant ethnic groups hell-bent for compensation from those innocent of former wrongs. Yet the grungy, black waif was right: the South is dead—the drawl gone, cotton fields and cornfields picked by machine. The scenes of darkies in the field, dragging cotton sacks is *gone with the wind*, as Margaret Mitchell wrote.

Often I wonder what happened to my world. It bears no resemblance to the world that I remember, with its old, seemingly contented blacks, the Burma Shave signs, pure country music, respect for the land and for each other—a cornucopia sufficient for most uses and gradual change. All that happens now is fast paced—almost frantic. No one seems satisfied with who they are or where they belong.

I suspect that this realization that the world had morphed was even more pronounced in the damn Depression. I think that I understand why Dad was traumatized by the event, but what I don't understand is why he was powerless to move on after it had run its course.

Now I see the country as a field overcome with locusts. We are too many for the land. It is an inescapable fact that because of our mismanagement and insatiable greed, the *air* and *water* have become our enemies. Already the elements of the ancients are embarking upon a terrible vengeance. Man will suffer an inglorious end, and his dry bones will rattle in the wind and lie bleached in the very fields that once grew King Cotton.

And so change is the common denominator of life. Mine is no exception, as it has been marked by incredible joys: a family I never thought I would have, moderate success in most of what I attempted in business, a reasonably long life punctuated by several brushes with death, and finally, at the end, a reluctant acceptance of that end. I am a man who tries to confront his demons head-on. Also, I did try to understand my motives in life, especially in light of this comment of Socrates: "The unexamined life is not worth living."

The lyric about the song of love being a song of woe blends into my life with the Emperor. Mother had her life marked with such sorrow and pain that it still haunts me. Change came and yet comes. It is the true certainty, for as the Buddhists say, all is impermanent and interdependent. Buddha also said that all is suffering.

The civil rights struggle is still ongoing, but now it seems as if there is a reversal of roles. I don't know how white people will be regarded in fifty years. I hesitate to consider what might occur.

I still long to be on the *water* or in the woods, to hear the wood duck call or the bellow of a gator or to catch a fat bluegill and remember the days with my kids. So blessed am I with my three children, all of whom have distinguished themselves in life and academics, and for my six grandchildren, taking positive steps, and for my wife, for her support and love through troubled times. It is a fact that my success in life is because of her. I think of what my son Lane said: "You get out of a relationship what you put into it." In all things in my life, I have found that to be true.

So many episodes I have left unwritten, simply because they are too painful to revisit. Some were with the Emperor, but most were with me running into a personal headwind. I do not handle change well, and the pace of advance astonishes me. Things obsolesce even before I can define them. My wife, children, and grandchildren are made of sterner stuff than I am. They will adjust, yeah, even embrace the whirlwind of change. I will only be further embarrassed if I stay much longer.

Nuts! All the chances for understanding between Dad and me are gone. I could never penetrate his space. It was my place to reach out, but I didn't. I remember that once he said something to the effect that we needed to get along. I made no overture. He began to cry. Have you ever seen an elderly man cry? I tell you—it is a sad sight. Damn it, I am sorry, and I wish I could reclaim that moment. He was an old man who was tormented, and I was a young man who was indifferent. I had built up an immunity to his hardened ways and unfortunately had developed my own.

I am a man of the past, an iconoclast comfortable with memory and historicity, content to remain as unfettered by change as possible. I am a self-taught man, and I have learned much about a wide range of topics, from medicine to law and even to Egyptian hieroglyphics and astrophysics. This and two degrees from respected universities are testaments to my love of knowledge. Everything I ever learned I used in thought or deed.

WARMTH

Mine has been a colorful life. I remember the ancient conception of the Three Fates in mythology. One spun the thread of a man's life, one measured the thread, and the last cut the thread. Thus did the Fates control how long a man would live. I thank the three of them, for my thread was long enough to complete much of what I envisioned. Uncle Redd once said that if a man lives his life to the fullest and tries to do his best in all his endeavors, he can feel warm inside.

This day I do feel warm inside. Most importantly, I think I will feel warm tomorrow, for, no matter the trial or pain to come, I made my best effort more often than not. And that effort is the final measure of a man.

Conclusion

There—it is done. A personality has been unraveled, dissected, and exposed, a character forged in the kiln of economic and civil strife, the Emperor, our absolute family monarch. When I think of him, I conjure up a lovely melody interrupted by clashing chords. Part of it was melody, the early years, and then came the pressure of economic stress and his desire to triumph at all costs.

We enjoyed cane-pole fishing for bream and hand-seining for bait, yet the majority of our time together was discord based on a simple disagreement about who would be the charioteer of my life, who would guide the white and black horses that represented my moods: him or me. Always the four elements would define me. I was a rugged, existential, iconoclastic, anachronistic, southern individualist who was always drawn to *water*. Twice it nearly killed me.

My relationship with my father was always tumultuous. There was *fire* in his eyes and in mine; never would there be peace between us. Seldom did we agree. The conception of a heaven, a perfect place, seemed hard for both of us to reconcile with the probes into space, even to Jupiter, Saturn, and maybe the Kuiper Belt and Oort cloud. When I learned that, in the early days, sailors feared sailing off the end of the earth, I could understand their fear. But now, with probes in all areas where the edges are hard to define, where is this magical place?

I did formulate a belief that was based on intent, not on actual observation, so I could dismiss the probes into space. Surely a benevolent God would intend that our focus be on him and the bounty we have received. Yet there was the age-old philosophical problem of evil. How can it be benevolent for a child to suffer horribly from cancer? Then science further complicated it with the fact that the universe is expanding. It would seem that as the redshift occurred, heaven would also be moving. I studied philosophy in an attempt to understand the grand plan. Now, near the old dirt nap, I admit I don't know. To truly appreciate the dilemma of the Fool on the precipice, one has to make a leap.

And one must wonder, if the *earth* was God's garden, why the hell he didn't he take better care of it?

That old, mean Depression forced my father into an early role as breadwinner for his mother and sisters. It made him a fighter. Against this backdrop of total immersion in self, his refusal to appreciate the arts, his lack of interest in any belief system other than himself, kept us at odds. Worse, his treatment of my dear mother wore hard on me and brought things to a boil. For both of us, faith was largely an inner strength.

His story and mine are now unveiled. Ours is a story of mistrust, misadventure, and disregard for others, in his case born of an economic horror and in mine of his shadow always as my shroud. I am an existentialist; I made my choices and take full responsibility for them. I plead my passionate love for freedom and my individuality, and I accept whatever judgment comes in whatever manner it may come. I did as I thought best for all concerned.

As for the combat between my father and me, I did seek some guidance, but none came. I felt a presence, not a direction; nothing more seemed evident. I am not blameless. Even now I recall the words of the existentialist Sartre (who won the Nobel Prize for Literature and refused it): "We have the war we deserve."